A level in a week

Psychology

David Putwain and Aidan Sammons, Abbey Tutorial College

Series editor: Kevin Byrne

Where to find the information you need

1.3
1.4

Letts Educational
Aldine Place
London W12 8AW
Tel: 0181 740 2266
Fax: 0181 743 8541
e-mail: mail@lettsed.co.uk
website: http://www.lettsed.co.uk

Every effort has been made to trace copyright holders and obtain their permission for the use of copyright material. The authors and publishers will gladly receive information enabling them to rectify any error or omission in subsequent editions.

First published 1999

Text © David Putwain and Aidan Sammons 1999
Design and illustration © BPP (Letts Educational) Ltd 1999

British Library Cataloguing in Publication Data
A CIP record for this book is available from the British Library.

ISBN 1 85758 9327

Editorial, design and production by Hart McLeod, Cambridge

Printed in Great Britain

Letts Educational is the trading name of BPP (Letts Educational) Ltd

Learning

Test your knowledge

10 minutes

1. An event which can be detected by an organism is called a _____. Behaviour produced by an organism as the result of a stimulus is called a _____.

2. Classical conditioning brings about a _____ between a stimulus and a response.

3. Classical conditioning assumes that organisms are _____ and only respond to stimuli.

4. Operant conditioning assumes that organisms are _____ and can produce new behaviours which are not conditioned responses. Whether or not a behaviour is repeated depends on the _____ it has for the organism.

5. If a behaviour is followed by a positive reinforcer then the organism is _____ likely to produce it in future. If a behaviour is followed by a _____ then the organism is less likely to produce it in future.

6. If a behaviour allows the organism to avoid a _____ _____ then the organism is more likely to produce it in future.

7. Operant conditioning is said to be deterministic, which means it suggests people do not have _____ _____.

8. Social Learning Theory proposes that people can learn by classical and operant conditioning and also by _____ other people. People whom we observe in order to learn new behaviours are called _____.

9. Whether a model's behaviour is imitated depends on several factors including the _____ of their behaviour and how _____ they are to the person observing them.

If you got them all right, skip to page 5

1

Learning

Improve your knowledge

20 minutes

1 **Classical conditioning** is a theory of learning which explains why organisms (including humans) learn to produce certain responses as a result of certain stimuli. Pavlov (1913) used conditioning to make dogs salivate to the sound of a bell.

2 Classical conditioning usually starts with an unconditioned reflex. This is a **stimulus-response (S-R)** connection which does not require learning. In the case of Pavlov's dogs it was the S-R connection which exists between seeing food (stimulus) and salivating (response). Pavlov rang a bell at the same time as presenting food to the dogs. The bell is called a **neutral stimulus** because it does not ordinarily result in a response from the dog. Once the bell and the food had been paired (presented together) a number of times, Pavlov found that the bell on its own could cause the dogs to salivate. We conclude that a new S-R connection had been made between the sound of the bell (now called the **conditioned stimulus**) and salivation (the **conditioned response**). The conditioning process can be described like this:

food (unconditioned stimulus – UCS) → salivation (unconditioned
                                      response – UCR)
food (UCS) + bell (neutral stimulus) → salivation (UCR)
bell (conditioned stimulus – CS)   → salivation (conditioned
                                      response – CR)

Watson and Rayner (1920) showed that humans can be conditioned by pairing a rat (neutral stimulus) with a loud, unpleasant noise (UCS) to produce a fear response (UCR). They used a small boy as their experimental participant; he developed a fear of the rat as a result of the conditioning.

Watson (1919) claimed that all learning could be explained using classical conditioning. He suggested that the socialisation process consisted of a large number of conditioning events in which people learn to produce certain responses as a result of certain stimuli.

3 There are a number of problems with this view. Firstly, classical conditioning starts with an unconditioned reflex, e.g. the connection between seeing food and salivating. In humans there are only a small number of these reflexes but the range of behaviours produced by humans is enormous. It seems unlikely that such a range of behaviour could arise from such a small number of reflexes. Secondly, classical conditioning assumes that an organism is passive. That is, all behaviour is a response which requires a stimulus in order to be produced. However, much behaviour is not a direct response to a stimulus but is produced spontaneously. Classical conditioning cannot explain why this happens.

4 B. F. Skinner (1938) proposed that whilst classical conditioning is one form of learning it is not the most important kind. He suggested that **operant conditioning** is more important. In operant conditioning, an organism's future behaviour depends on the consequences of its past behaviour. For example, if a rat pushes a lever (behaviour) and is given a piece of food (consequence) then it is more likely to press the lever again in future. Skinner said that the consequence of a behaviour can take one of three forms:

5 If behaviour is followed by a positive reinforcement then it is likely to be repeated in future, e.g. a rat pushes a lever and is given food. If a behaviour is followed by a punishment then it is less likely to be repeated in future, e.g. a rat pushes a lever and is given an electric shock.

6 If a behaviour allows the organism to avoid a negative reinforcer then it is likely to be repeated, e.g. a rat avoids an electric shock by pushing a lever.

Skinner and others suggested that people learn behaviours mainly through operant conditioning and **shaping**. Shaping is a process in which successively closer approximations of a desired behaviour are reinforced. For example, Skinner suggested that language begins to be acquired when parents reinforce, e.g. with praise etc., infants for any vocalisation. Once the child has started vocalising, parents only reinforce those sounds which resemble actual words. Eventually, through selective reinforcement, the child learns the vocabulary and grammar of its language.

7 Many researchers have disagreed with Skinner. Brown et al. (1969) found that parents do not selectively reinforce children for grammatically correct statements. This means that operant conditioning cannot explain how language is acquired. Skinner's theory is also deterministic (it does not allow for **free will**). Skinner claimed that free will was an illusion and that all behaviour is controlled by a person's reinforcement history.

8 The **Social Learning Theory** is based on operant conditioning but allows for people to learn by observing others. The person who is observed and copied is called a **model**. Whether or not people copy a model's behaviour depends on the consequences it has for the model. For example, if a child sees someone being reinforced for aggressive behaviour it is likely to produce that behaviour itself.

9 A person is more likely to imitate a model's behaviour if they perceive the model to be similar to themselves. Bandura (1973) demonstrated observational learning by exposing children to images of adults behaving aggressively towards a doll. The adult was either reinforced (praised) or punished (told off) by another adult. When the children were allowed access to a similar doll, those who had seen the adult reinforced were far more likely to reproduce the aggressive behaviours they had seen.

Now learn how to use your knowledge

Learning

Use your knowledge

30 minutes

Hints

1 Describe the process of classical conditioning.

2 How would classical conditioning explain why a person developed a phobia of dogs after being bitten?

3 What criticisms can be made of the idea that all behaviour is acquired through classical conditioning?

4 Explain the difference between classical and operant conditioning.

5 Explain the difference between punishment and negative reinforcement.

6 What is shaping?

7 How would operant conditioning explain how phobias are maintained?

8 How would you use Social Learning Theory to reduce aggression in society?

what happened in Watson and Rayner's (1921) study?

what can classical conditioning not explain?

one of them makes a behaviour more likely, one less likely

how did Skinner describe language acquisition?

negative reinforcement

what is the most efficient way to use observational learning?

Answers on page 66

Perception

Test your knowledge

10 minutes

1. The visual cliff study found that young infants would not crawl on the 'deep' side. This suggests that depth perception is _____.

2. The Gestalt psychologists believed that one innate feature of our visual perception is organisation into _____ (foreground) and ground (everything else).

3. We see objects as the same size and shape (size and shape constancy) despite the fact that the same object can throw very different _____ images.

4. Pattern recognition depends upon matching visual information with information stored in the _____.

5. Gibson's (1979) Theory of Perception argues that _____ information is much more useful in perception.

6. Gregory's (1972) theory suggests that perception is more of a mental _____ since the information presented to our senses is generally poor.

7. Niesser's (1976) model solves the problem of using exclusively top-down or bottom-up information by suggesting they are both used in a perceptual _____.

8. Cross-cultural studies suggest that the _____ may play an important role in perception.

Answers

If you got them all right, skip to page 9

Perception

Improve your knowledge

20 minutes

1   The idea behind the study of **perceptual development** is to try to identify which aspects of perception are innate and which aspects require learning. Different types of studies have been designed to answer the question. The obvious starting point is human infants, since they have little opportunity for learning so any perceptual abilities they possess must be innate. The disadvantage is trying to infer what they can and can't do from their behaviour, since we cannot ask them. Some studies like the visual cliff (Gibson and Walk, 1960) appear to show that depth perception is innate, but actually used infants aged six months old and so there was opportunity for learning.

2   The **Gestalt** psychologists of the 1920s and 1930s identified one of the most basic innate features of our organisation of visual perception, that what we tend to focus on stands forward (**figure** or foreground) and everything else stands back (**ground**). The Rubins vase (1915) is a good example of this. Koffka (1935) developed several laws which determine whether we see something which will form figure or ground. Dallenbach's (1951) fragmentary picture ignores these rules which is why it is so hard to see.

3   When an object presents a large retinal image to us we tend to perceive a large object close up. If the retinal size of that object decreases then this can mean one of two things. Either the object is decreasing in size and staying in the same place or the object is moving away from us and staying the same size. If we are familiar with objects in our environment and have learnt what size they are, we will perceive them as moving away from us rather than getting smaller. This is referred to as **size constancy** – that we see the object as staying the same size even though the retinal size is changing.

4 Theories of **pattern recognition** try to account for how we match up a visual stimulus of an object with a memory of that object. The one thing they all have in common is that they are all bottom-up and do not take into account of how context and surroundings may affect how we recognise objects.

5 Gibson's (1979) **Theory of Perception** believes that the visual information we receive is of a high quality and so we can gain information about what the world is like directly from our senses without having to make reference to stored information (a bottom-up theory).

6 Gregory (1972) argues that the information presented to our senses is ambiguous and uses evidence from visual illusions to support his view. He believes that perception is a process of filling in the gaps left by sensory information and the information used in this process comes from memory (a top-down theory).

7 Niesser (1976) managed to combine the two approaches successfully. Bottom-up processes sample some of the available sensory information which are then used to build up stored models of what the world is like. These stored models then act in a top-down fashion to direct which sensory information is sampled.

8 Early cross-cultural studies compared different cultures on their susceptibility to various visual illusions. Some studies found differences, some contradictory and others no differences. Most studies that found differences tended to attribute the ecology (the physical environment where we live) as determining susceptibility to illusions. This led Segall et al. (1966) to propose the 'carpentered world hypothesis' which suggests that people who live in a culture with much geometry (straight lines, right angles, etc.) will be more prone to certain illusions, such as the Müller-Lyer illusion, and other cultures will be more prone to other illusions. The implication is that ecology can actually affect the way in which we see the world.

Now learn how to use your knowledge

Perception

Use your knowledge

1. Are there any other approaches to the study of perceptual development in addition to the human infant as the participant?

2. Is depth perception innate or learnt?

3. What are the limitations of the Gestalt approach?

4. How has Gregory (1972) explained the Müller-Lyer illusion in terms of misapplied size constancy?

5. What is Marr's model of perception/pattern recognition?

6. Assess the experimental evidence for cross-cultural differences in perception.

maturing children and animals

what are the methodological limitations of the studies?

do the Gestalt laws cover all possibilities?

where do we see the shape of the Müller-Lyer illusion under real life circumstances?

think of computer analogies

what are the methodological difficulties?

Answers on page 66

Memory

Test your knowledge

10 minutes

1. The _____-store model suggests that memory is broken down into a sensory-buffer store (SBS), the short-term memory (STM) and the long-term memory (LTM).

2. Miller (1956) claimed that the STM capacity for an average person was _____ units, plus or minus two.

3. The depth of processing model suggests that whether we remember things for a long time or not depends on whether we elaborate on the _____ of material.

4. A higher degree of organisation in LTM results in a _____ amount of information recalled.

5. Freud believed that forgetting was due to material being _____ in the unconscious part of the mind.

6. Proactive interference is where _____ learning interferes with later learning.

7. _____ are devices that enable us to remember long lists of unrelated items by imposing organisation on material which contains none.

8. The reconstructive nature of memory is a problem for the eyewitnesses of crimes because what they remember may be changed by how _____ are asked by police and lawyers.

Answers

Memory

Improve your knowledge

20 minutes

1 Although there have been many different models of memory developed, there are three which are of central importance:

- the multi-store model
- the depth of processing model
- the working memory model.

The **multi-store model** breaks down memory into three parts. The SBS holds an imprint of information presented to senses for a short period of time (approximately 1–2 seconds for auditory information).

2 We pay attention to some of this information entering the STM which can hold information for up to 30 seconds. If we do not rehearse this information it will be displaced from STM. Through rehearsal, some of this information enters LTM which is presumed to have an unlimited capacity.

3 The **depth of processing model** does not break memory down into separate short- and long-term memory stores in order to account for why we remember some information for a long time and some for only a short time. Instead, the length of time that we remember something is dependent on how well we learn it, or to be more specific what type of processing is being used at the time of learning. Type one (**maintenance**) **rehearsal** does not lead to long memories but type two (**elaborative**) **rehearsal** does because it involves a semantic processing or a processing of information for meaning.

4 It is only because our memories are so well organised that we are capable of remembering so much information. It is usually assumed that our LTM is organised in chunks of items which are related or have a similar meaning. Eysenck (1977) demonstrated how information is organised into categorical clusters. These are like headings (such as sports) which contain lists of related information (such as tennis, cricket, golf, soccer, etc).

5 Freud believed in **motivated forgetting,** where information which has a high painful, emotional, anxiety-ridden association is pushed into the unconscious part of the mind. This may help to explain certain aspects of forgetting in special conditions but lab studies often show no evidence for this. However, for ethical reasons they cannot produce traumatic phenomena to see if people will repress them.

6 The **Interference Theory** is that similar memories compete with one another and the result is that forgetting occurs. Many lab studies show evidence in favour of the interference theory, but this is a classic case where lack of ecological validity is the problem.

7 **Mnemonics** are techniques invented by the Greeks to aid memory. The reason why they work is that they impose organisation on information which lacks structure. The existing memories act like pegs and you hang the new information on these pegs. This method is used by world memory champions to remember long lists of unrelated items. So while this technique may be good for remembering things like shopping lists, it is of little use for exams where understanding is the essential factor that aids recall.

8 Far more serious is the issue of eyewitnesses to crimes. As Bartlett (1932) showed, our memories are prone to reconstructing events. So what we remember may not be what actually happened but what we *think* may have happened. Loftus showed in a series of lab experiments in the 1970s that our memory of crucial details may distort depending on how the questions were phrased. This implies that police or lawyers may skilfully make use of leading questions in order to influence the memory of the witness, but other studies have suggested that the effect is not as great in real-life circumstances. A technique used to guard against this, based on the theory of context dependent forgetting, is the **cognitive interview**.

Memory

Use your knowledge

1 What is the evidence for the multi-store model?

2 What advantages does the working model have over the STM (as described in the multi-store model)?

3 Does organising information have an effect on retrieval of information?

4 How do we organise larger chunks of information into memory?

5 What other popular theories of forgetting exist?

6 What are the advantages and disadvantages of studying memory in the lab versus studying it in real-life settings?

7 Is eyewitness testimony reliable?

Hints

anterograde amnesia, the serial-position effect
active versus passive processing

why are mnemonics so effective?

schematic processing

trace decay and cue-dependent

ecological validity versus experimental control

lab versus real-life studies

Answers on page 67

Cognitive development

10 minutes

Test your knowledge

1. Cognitive development concerns the way a child's ability to _____ develops with age.

2. Piaget proposed that a child's knowledge is organised into _____ into which new knowledge can be integrated by _____ or _____.

3. The four stages of development in Piaget's theory are: _____, _____, _____ _____ and _____ _____.

4. A pre-operational child cannot take the perspective of another person. This is called _____ thought.

5. It has been suggested that cognitive development is more _____ than Piaget's stage theory suggests.

6. Vygotsky also proposed a Stage Theory of Cognitive Development but thought that Piaget had underestimated the role of _____ and _____ _____.

7. Vygotsky's stages are the _____ _____, _____, _____ _____ and _____ _____ stages.

8. If the child is brought to the zone of potential development it can fulfil its cognitive _____.

9. In peer teaching, a _____ able child assists a _____ able one.

10. Both Piaget and Vygotsky have been very influential in _____.

Answers

1 reason 2 schemas, assimilation, accommodation
3 sensorimotor, preoperational, concrete operational, formal
operational 4 egocentric 5 gradual 6 language, social
interaction 7 vague syncretic, complexes, potential concept,
mature concept 8 potential 9 more, less 10 education

If you got them all right, skip to page 18

14

Cognitive development

Improve your knowledge

20 minutes

1 **Cognitive development** concerns the way a child's ability to think and reason develops with age. Piaget proposed that cognitive development is neither wholly due to maturation nor just the result of experience. He suggested that intelligence develops as a result of the interaction between biological and environmental factors.

2 Piaget suggested that children develop their abilities through interacting with the world around them. Their knowledge is organised into **schemas** which are representations of all the child knows about a particular object, person or situation. When new experiences are encountered they must be made to fit in with the child's schemas. This can happen in two ways:

- **assimilation** – new knowledge can be fitted into existing schemas
- **accommodation** – if this cannot be done, the schemas must be extended or changed so that the experience can be fitted in.

3 Piaget proposed that children go through an ordered sequence of **developmental stages**. At each stage, the child's way of thinking about the world has certain key characteristics.

See the table on the following page.

Piaget's developmental stages

Stage	Main features
Sensorimotor 0–2 years	Infants obtain knowledge through experiencing and acting on the world. Object permanence develops: the child understands that objects continue to exist even though they are out of sight.
Pre-operational 2–7 years	Child can use mental symbols to think about the world but cognitive capacities are still limited. The child's thought is egocentric (it cannot take the perspective of another person) and it has difficulty classifying objects.
Concrete operational 7–11 years	The child develops mental rules (operations) for thinking about the world (e.g. adding, subtracting). This allows the child to classify objects and recognise logical relations between them.
Formal operational 11+ years	The child becomes capable of fully abstract thought and can solve problems in a logical, systematic way.

4 Piaget devised a number of tasks to assess children's cognitive abilities and stage of development. For example, in the 'three mountains' test for egocentricity, the child is shown a model of three mountains on which a doll is placed. When asked what the doll can see, a pre-operational child will typically describe what he or she can see.

5 Piaget believed that the stages are relatively discrete and that children switch between them quite suddenly. However, it has been suggested that children's cognitive abilities develop more steadily than Piaget suggests. It is also possible that the difficulty of some of Piaget's tasks led him to underestimate children's abilities. On modified versions of Piaget's tasks, children tend to show higher cognitive abilities at a younger age.

6 Vygotsky proposed that Piaget had underestimated the role of language and social interaction in cognitive development. He suggested that children develop their cognitive abilities through interacting with adults and older children. Language is important because it provides a powerful set of tools for developing concepts.

7 Vygotsky also believed that cognitive development proceeds in stages with key characteristics.

Vygotsky's developmental stages

Stage	Main features
Vague syncretic stage	The child solves problems through trial and error with little or no real understanding.
Complexes stage	Problems are solved with some use of strategies.
Potential concept stage	The child can deal with a problem by focusing on one aspect at a time.
Mature stage	The child can deal with several aspects of a concept problem simultaneously.

8 Vygotsky believed that, with support from adults, the child could be brought into the 'zone of potential development', where the child is able to fulfil its current cognitive potential and begin to stretch its abilities.

9 Vygotsky also advocated educational strategies such as **peer teaching**, in which a more advanced child assists a less advanced one. Both children learn from this process, the less advanced one by having its ability stretched, the more advanced one by having its skills consolidated.

10 Although Vygotsky produced little evidence to support his theories, much research was carried out by Bruner who was able to validate many of Vygotsky's ideas. The theory has been highly influential in educational practice (as has Piaget's). Even though the theories conflict to some extent, it has also proven possible to apply the insights of each to develop successful teaching strategies.

Now learn how to use your knowledge

Cognitive development

30 minutes

Use your knowledge

Hints

1 Describe Piaget's Theory of Cognitive Development.

schemas and stages

2 How would you test for object permanence in an infant?

you need a non-verbal test

3 Summarise the main criticisms of Piaget's theory and methodology.

4 Describe Vygotsky's Theory of Cognitive Development.

see table on p. 17

5 Contrast Piaget's and Vygotsky's views of the developing child.

what role do other people play in the child's development?

6 How would Piaget and Vygotsky differ in their application to education?

Answers on page 68

Moral development

10 minutes

Test your knowledge

1 Piaget suggests that a child's moral development is linked to its _____ development.

2 Piaget suggests that children go through four stages of moral development, the _____, _____ _____, _____ and _____ _____ stages.

3 A child's stage of moral development can be ascertained by examining the _____ it makes about moral dilemmas.

4 Piaget's theory does not seem to apply outside Western society. It is therefore _____ _____.

5 Additionally, the difficulty of Piaget's research tasks may have led him to _____ children's abilities.

6 Learning Theory proposes that moral behaviour is acquired through _____ and _____ conditioning.

7 Social Learning Theory also stresses the importance of _____ learning.

8 Learning Theory is not culture bound, since a child's eventual moral behaviour depends on its _____ and _____.

9 However, Learning Theories can be criticised because they underestimate the role of _____ in moral behaviour.

Answers

1 cognitive **2** premoral, moral realist, transition, moral reciprocity **3** judgements **4** culture bound **5** underestimate **6** classical, operant **7** observational **8** society, culture **9** cognition

 If you got them all right, skip to page 23

Moral development

Improve your knowledge

20 minutes

1 Piaget suggests that a child's **moral development** is linked to its **cognitive development**. The higher a child's stage of cognitive development, the greater its ability to make reasoned decisions about what is right and wrong.

2 Piaget suggests that the child goes through four stages of moral development:

Stage	Age	Main features
Premoral	0–3 years	The child does not grasp the idea of rules, so moral reasoning is impossible.
Moral realism (Heteronomous)	3–7 years	The child regards rules as absolute and unchangeable. Actions are judged according to the severity of their consequences.
Transition	7–11 years	Elements of moral realism and moral reciprocity are combined.
Moral reciprocity (Autonomous)	11+ years	The child realises that rules exist only by agreement and can be changed. Actions are judged according to the intention of the actor.

3 Piaget tested his theory by examining the responses made by children to scenarios which required **moral reasoning**. In one study, children were told two stories: in the first, a boy accidentally breaks fifteen cups, in the second the boy breaks one cup whilst trying to steal some jam. The children were asked which boy was naughtier. Younger children (stage two) tended to say the first was naughtier since the consequences of his action were more severe. Older children (stage three) judged the second boy more harshly since he was intending to do something wrong. This is in line with Piaget's prediction.

4 Although Piaget's theory is well supported by research studies on Western children, there is less evidence to support it in other cultures. Because the theory does not apply universally it is said to be **culture bound**, i.e. it applies only in a particular culture.

5 As with his work on cognitive development, it is also possible that Piaget has underestimated the moral abilities of younger children. In his original research, the children had the stories read out to them. This may have led to confusion resulting in poorer performance. Chandler et al. (1973) presented the stories as short films and found that six year-olds were able to understand the boys' intentions and use this as the basis for their judgement.

6 The **Learning Theory of Moral Development** stresses the role of **classical** and **operant conditioning** and observational learning in moral behaviour.

Behaviourists suggest that when a child is punished for doing something wrong, the result is anxiety. This anxiety becomes linked with the misdeed through classical conditioning, leading to anxiety when similar acts are contemplated. Through operant conditioning the child tends to avoid actions which have led to punishment in the past and alternative behaviours, which do not result in punishment, are strengthened (negative reinforcement).

7 The **Social Learning Theory** proposes that children acquire moral behaviour mainly through observing models. If a child sees a model being punished for certain behaviours then they are unlikely to imitate them; conversely, children are likely to imitate the behaviours they see reinforced in others.

8 Learning Theories of moral development have the major advantage of not being culture bound. They stress that the set of moral behaviours a child eventually learns will depend on what is considered acceptable within that child's culture.

9 A significant disadvantage of Learning Theories is that they tend not to consider the role of **cognition** in moral behaviour. Although Piaget underestimated the moral abilities of children, he was probably right to believe that reasoning is a major factor in the decisions people make about how to act.

Moral development

Use your knowledge

1   Describe Piaget's Cognitive Theory of Moral Development.

2   Contrast the Cognitive and Learning Theory approaches to moral development.

3   To what extent is Piaget's approach supported by evidence?

4   Using classical and operant conditioning, describe how parents might shape the moral behaviour of their children.

5   Why does Social Learning Theory give a better account of moral development than classical and operant conditioning?

6   Are the Cognitive and Learning Theory approaches to moral development necessarily opposed to each other?

Answers on page 68

Evolutionary principles and behaviour

10 minutes

Test your knowledge

1 Any behaviour will have some inherited components, referred to as phylogeny, and some learned components referred to as _____.

2 Fixed action patterns refer to behaviours which are _____.

3 Animals displaying fitness possess characteristics which enable them to _____ more successfully.

4 Altruism is behaviour that shows an unselfish concern for _____ with no obvious advantage for oneself.

5 A _____ relationship is one where two individual animals carry out mutually beneficial acts because of the benefit they receive in return.

6 Sociobiological theories of human behaviour are those which seek to explain human behaviour from an _____ perspective.

7 Evolutionary theories of helping behaviour in humans suggest that we help strangers because we may share similar _____ to them.

Answers

 If you got them all right, skip to page 27

Evolutionary principles and behaviour

20 minutes

Improve your knowledge

1   One of the difficulties facing researchers in the field of animal behaviour is determining the extent to which a behaviour is learnt or inherited. Inevitably most behaviours have elements of both, but it is important to remember that behaviours which are learnt have not come from a vacuum but that the animal must have been 'ripe' to learn and are modifications of an **innate behaviour**. For example, blue tits have learnt to open the tops of milk-bottles, but this is only a slight modification of their innate behaviour where they strip the bark from trees to feed on insects living underneath (Sherry and Galef, 1984). The only way to assess innate and learnt components of behaviour is by careful observation of a species over a long period of time.

2   Inherited behaviours are referred to as **fixed action patterns** and have several defining characteristics such as being stereotyped, universal and species-specific. That is, for a particular species an innate behaviour will appear in the same way for all members of that species. Another feature of innate behaviours is that they are all triggered by the same stimuli. A good example of a fixed action pattern studied by Tinbergen and Perdeck (1950) is how herring-gulls feed their chicks. The infant gulls actually respond to the colour of the adult's beak and the contrast in colour between the beak and a small spot on the beak to produce a begging behaviour. The adult gulls respond to the behaviour by regurgitating food for the chicks to feed on.

3   Certain behaviours and morphology enable an individual to mate more successfully than others. These individuals will produce more offspring and so their genetic characteristics expressed in behaviour and morphology will become more prevalent over several generations.

4 Darwin initially had problems explaining why individuals who displayed **altruistic** behaviour and individuals whose body morphology displayed no obvious advantage did not die out, because these characteristics have no apparent fitness. Subsequent researchers have also discovered that apparently altruistic behaviour may actually be selfish when viewed on a genetic level, referred to as the '**paradox of altruism**'.

5 Sometimes individuals who are not genetically related and even of different species carry out altruistic behaviours – this is a **symbiotic relationship**. For example, small cleaner fish eat parasites on the scales of sharks whilst feeding on scraps of food. There is an evolutionary advantage to the cleaner fish who has no other food source and to the shark for whom parasites are a significant health risk. However, it must be remembered that each individual is actually acting in their own self-interest and that these are only behaviour patterns where a helping relationship has evolved because of **adaptation** and **fitness**.

6 Evolutionary principles have also been applied to what have traditionally been areas of social psychology (often referred to as **sociobiological theories**), two of which are **helping behaviour** and **romantic attraction**. As the evolutionary bandwagon gains momentum, there are evolutionary explanations for human behaviours of ever increasing complexity, such as the ability to spot liars.

7 The evolutionary explanation for pro-social behaviour (Rushton, 1989) suggests that we only help others who share similar genetic material to ourselves. The problem with this explanation is, whilst it may explain why we help family members, it does not explain why we help strangers. Evolutionary theorists propose that we can assess the genetic similarity of ourselves to others through superficial appearances, but there is no evidence for this.

✔ *Now learn how to use your knowledge*

Evolutionary principles and behaviour

30 minutes

Use your knowledge

Hints

1 What is meant by an animal being 'ripe' to learn?

why are rats but not pigeons easily conditioned to food aversions?

2 Is the fixed action pattern a good explanation for behaviour?

what are the exceptions to the rule?

3 What is the paradox of altruism?

altruistic behaviour versus selfish genes

4 What is ritualised aggression?

how might fitness be linked to fighting?

5 How have predator–prey relationships co-evolved?

running speed vs. hiding

6 How do animals compete for resources?

herbivores vs. carnivores, territorial vs. non-territorial

7 What is the evolutionary explanation for human mate selection?

what are the different strategies used by men and women?

Answers on page 69

Basic biological processes

Test your knowledge

1 The nervous system can be divided into the _____ , _____ and _____ nervous systems.

2 The central nervous system consists of the _____ and the _____ .

3 The ANS has two divisions, the _____ and _____ branches.

4 When a threatening stimulus is encountered, the sympathetic ANS becomes active. This is called the _____ or _____ response.

5 The endocrine system consists of a number of _____ which secrete _____ .

6 The process by which an organism maintains a stable internal environment is called _____ . Homeostatic mechanisms are mediated by the _____ .

7 In thermo-regulation, blood temperature is monitored in the _____ area of the hypothalamus.

8 Besides physiological mechanisms, organisms can also use _____ to regulate temperature.

Answers

1 central, peripheral, autonomic   2 brain, spinal cord
3 sympathetic, parasympathetic   4 fight, flight
5 glands, hormones   6 homeostasis, hypothalamus
7 pre-optic   8 behaviour

 If you got them all right, skip to page 33

28

Basic biological processes

Improve your knowledge

1 The nervous system can be divided into the **central**, **peripheral** and **autonomic nervous systems** (CNS, PNS and ANS). The CNS deals with processing of information, the PNS with the external environment (sensing and moving) and the ANS with the internal environment (internal regulation and homeostasis).

2 The CNS is divided into the brain and the spinal cord. The spinal cord mainly serves the purpose of transmitting messages between the brain and the PNS. The brain is subdivided into the hindbrain, midbrain and forebrain.

	Major structures of interest	Main functions
Hindbrain	Pons Medulla	Relaying messages to other parts of the brain, basic survival functions.
	Cerebellum	Fine motor control, posture and balance.
Midbrain		Processing sensory information (hearing, vision etc.).
Forebrain	Hypothalamus	Co-ordinating CNS, ANS and endocrine activity, homeostasis.
	Limbic system	Emotion and arousal, aspects of learning and memory.
	Cortex	Higher cognitive functions; language, thought, planning, problem solving, learning, memory.

3 The ANS has two divisions, the **sympathetic** and **parasympathetic ANS**, which work in opposition to each other. When activity increases in one branch it decreases in the other. When the body is expending large amounts of energy, activity increases in the sympathetic branch. As a result of this, heart and respiration rate increase and digestive activity slows down. When energy is being conserved, activity increases in the parasympathetic branch and the opposite happens.

The autonomic nervous system

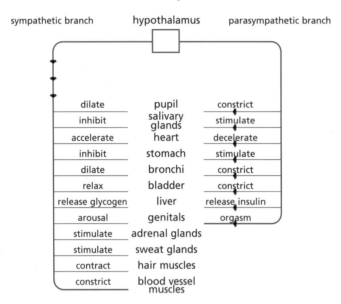

sympathetic branch	hypothalamus	parasympathetic branch
dilate	pupil	constrict
inhibit	salivary glands	stimulate
accelerate	heart	decelerate
inhibit	stomach	stimulate
dilate	bronchi	constrict
relax	bladder	constrict
release glycogen	liver	release insulin
arousal	genitals	orgasm
stimulate	adrenal glands	
stimulate	sweat glands	
contract	hair muscles	
constrict	blood vessel muscles	

4 When faced with a threatening stimulus, the sympathetic ANS becomes active in a pattern of changes called the **fight or flight response**. Heart and respiration rate rise, digestion and salivation are inhibited, glucose is released into the blood and the surface blood vessels dilate. This is to prepare the organism for physical exertion: more oxygen is taken into the blood and is diverted to the skeletal muscles where it is needed most; glucose is released to provide fuel. Digestion and related activity is inhibited because it is not required.

5 The **endocrine system** consists of a number of glands situated around the body which release various hormones into the bloodstream. Hormones are chemical messengers which act on the organs and tissues of the body to bring about changes in the way they function.

Some endocrine glands and hormones

Endocrine gland	Hormones released	Effect on body
Pituitary	Growth hormone Various others	Tissue growth. Stimulate other endocrine glands to secrete hormones.
Gonads	Oestrogen Testosterone	Sexual development, muscle growth.
Thyroid	Thyroxin	Increases metabolic rate.
Adrenal cortex	Corticosteroids	Release glucose for energy expenditure. Depress immune response.
Adrenal medulla	Adrenaline	Activates sympathetic branch of ANS.

6 **Homeostasis** is the mechanism by which an organism maintains a constant internal environment. Metabolic functioning can only take place within a strictly limited range of conditions (temperature, amount of water, presence of fuel etc.). Homeostatic mechanisms work on a negative feedback principle; current conditions within the body are monitored and when they approach predetermined limits, mechanisms are triggered which correct them. Homeostatic functions involve the CNS, ANS and endocrine system working in co-ordination. The activity of the three systems is mediated through the hypothalamus, which is situated in the CNS and connected to the ANS and pituitary gland.

7 Temperature regulation is an example of a **homeostatic function**. The human body maintains a core temperature of 37.2° Celsius. The temperature of the blood is monitored by receptors in the pre-optic hypothalamus. When the blood temperature rises, the sympathetic ANS causes sweating to increase and the endocrine system releases less thyroxin, slowing down the rate of metabolism and thereby decreasing heat production. When the blood is too cool, the sympathetic ANS causes shivering, which generates heat and causes the body hairs to erect, reducing heat loss. At the same time, more thyroxin is released, increasing the rate of metabolism.

8 Besides these physiological mechanisms, humans also have a number of behavioural strategies available for regulating temperature. For example, if we are too hot, we can move to a cooler place, open a window or remove some clothing. Generally, the more behavioural strategies an organism has available, the less it relies on physiological mechanisms (Kalat, 1998).

Now learn how to use your knowledge

Basic biological processes

30 minutes

Use your knowledge

Hints

1   Describe the structure of the nervous system.

2   Outline the structure and functions of the ANS.

the ANS is involved in a wide range of functions

3   In what ways do the effects of the endocrine system differ from those of the nervous system?

how are endocrine messages sent?

4   Explain what is meant by the term 'homeostasis'.

use examples

5   Assess the role of the CNS, ANS and endocrine system in one homeostatic function.

show how they work together

✓ Answers on page 70

Sleep and dreaming

Test your knowledge

10 minutes

1. The sleep-wake cycle is an example of a _____ rhythm.

2. In mammals, sleep is regulated by the pineal gland, which produces _____. The pineal is in turn regulated by the _____ _____.

3. The sleep-wake cycle is synchronised with the night-day cycle by means of specialised _____ in the retina.

4. Sleep has five stages. Stages three and four are called _____ _____ _____. Dreams seem to occur in _____ sleep.

5. Prolonged sleep deprivation may result in mild _____ and cognitive _____.

6. Evolutionary theories suggest that sleep evolved because it gives animals a _____ advantage.

7. The Psychodynamic Theory of Dreams suggests they originate in the _____ mind.

8. The Psychodynamic Theory is regarded as _____ by many psychologists.

9. The Activation-Synthesis Theory of Dreams suggests they are a _____ of brain activity during REM sleep.

10. However, because dreams cannot be _____ examined, this theory must still be considered _____.

Answers

1 circadian 2 melatonin, supra-chiasmatic nucleus 3 photo-receptors 4 slow wave sleep, REM 5 hallucinations, deficits 6 survival 7 unconscious 8 unscientific 9 by-product 10 objectively, untestable

Sleep and dreaming

Improve your knowledge

20 minutes

1 The **sleep-wake** cycle is a **circadian** rhythm, which means it goes through one cycle every 24 hours. Most people sleep for eight hours in every 24. The sleep-wake cycle is governed by internal factors, called **endogenous pacemakers** and external factors, called **zeitgebers**.

2 Sleep is controlled by the pineal gland, which secretes a hormone called **melatonin**. Melatonin acts on the sleep centres in the brain to induce sleep. The pineal gland in birds and reptiles is light sensitive. Because their skulls are thin, daylight (a zeitgeber) can penetrate the skull and act on the pineal, inhibiting melatonin production. When melatonin production is inhibited, the animal wakes up.

Mammals have thicker skulls, so the light cannot penetrate to act on the pineal gland. In mammals the sleep-wake cycle is controlled by the supra-chiasmatic nucleus (SCN), which generates an internal rhythm, regulating the production of melatonin by the pineal gland. The SCN is therefore the body's main **endogenous pacemaker**.

3 Daylight deprivation studies show that the SCN generates a rhythm which varies over a period of longer than 24 hours. Therefore the SCN requires 'resetting' each day since otherwise the body's sleep-wake cycle would eventually become desynchronised with the night-day cycle. Resynchronisation is made possible by specialised photo-receptors in the retina, connected to the SCN. These react to low levels of daylight, allowing the internally generated rhythm of the SCN to be synchronised with the external zeitgeber of the day-night cycle.

4 There are five different types of sleep which can be distinguished by electro-encephalograph (EEG) readings. The brain moves in cycles between the five stages several times during an eight hour sleep period. Stages one and two represent light sleep. Stages three and four are deep sleep (called **slow wave sleep** or SWS) and stage five is **REM** sleep. About five times a night the brain enters **rapid eye movement** (REM) sleep. During REM the skeletal muscles are paralysed and the EEG reading resembles that of a waking person. Dreams seem to occur during REM sleep.

Sleep deprivation studies show that SWS is the most important type of sleep, followed by REM sleep. A person deprived of sleep for a long period will recover most of their SWS and about a third of their REM (this is called **REM rebound**). Stages one and two are thought to be relatively unimportant since sleep-deprived people recover little of these sleep types.

5 **Restoration Theories of Sleep** suggest that SWS and REM are required to repair the body's tissues (SWS) and replenish levels of neurotransmitters (REM). Support for this view comes from the findings that animals deprived of sleep eventually die. Prolonged sleep deprivation in humans results in depression of the immune system. Deprivation of REM sleep in humans results in mild hallucinations and deficits in cognitive functioning which further supports the view that REM is necessary for normal brain functioning.

6 **Evolutionary Theories of Sleep** suggest that it evolved because it confers a survival advantage. Whilst asleep, animals expend less energy because they are not moving and their body temperature drops. This fits in with the finding that small animals, e.g. mice, who lose heat at a great rate, sleep for a greater proportion of the day than large animals, e.g. cows, who lose heat much slower.

Evolutionary theory also predicts that vulnerable prey animals, who must be constantly vigilant, will sleep for much shorter periods than animals with no predators. This prediction is also supported by comparing the average sleep times of the fox (9.8 hours) with that of the sheep (3.8 hours). Although they live in similar environments, the predator can afford to sleep for much longer than the prey.

7 The **Psychodynamic Theory of Dreams** suggests that they are a form of unconscious wish-fulfilment. The remembered (manifest) content of a dream is a symbolic representation of unconscious desires (the latent content). These desires must appear in a disguised form as they are unacceptable to the conscious mind.

8 The Psychodynamic Theory cannot be directly tested since the unconscious mind cannot be objectively examined. The latent content of dreams can only be accessed via psychoanalysis, which is viewed with suspicion by many psychologists since it relies heavily on the subjective interpretations of the analyst. Many psychologists therefore view the psychodynamic theory of dreams as unscientific.

9 The **Activation-Synthesis Theory of Dreams** suggests that the brain requires REM sleep for normal functioning. One effect of REM is the firing of large numbers of neurones in the cerebral cortex (activation). It is suggested that, since the firing of cortical neurones usually accompanies waking experience, the cognitive system interprets neuronal firing during REM as real experiences. However, since the firing is seemingly random, the experiences are not coherent. In order to make sense of these apparent experiences during REM, the cognitive system synthesises them into a coherent whole (the remembered content of the dream).

10 The Activation-Synthesis Theory of Dreams fits in with what we know about what is happening in the brain during REM and is considered more scientific by most psychologists. However, since psychologists:

- are unable to examine people's dreams directly
- have relatively little idea of how brain activity corresponds to subjective experience

the theory must still be considered speculative. We currently have no way of deciding whether it is true or not.

Sleep and dreaming

Use your knowledge

30 minutes

Hints

1 Describe the sleep system in birds, reptiles and mammals.

2 How could we confirm that the endogenous rhythm of the SCN is longer than 24 hours?

why are the sleep-wake and night-day cycles usually synchronised?

3 Why do psychologists believe that dreams occur during REM sleep?

the EEG can help here

4 Compare and contrast the Evolutionary and Restoration Theories of Sleep.

point out the similarities and differences

5 Does either the Evolutionary or the Restoration Theory have to be right?

are they opposed or complementary?

6 Why is the Psychodynamic Theory of Dreams considered unscientific?

what sort of evidence do scientists require?

7 Could the same criticism be levelled at the Activation-Synthesis Theory?

Answers on page 70

Conformity and obedience

10 minutes

Test your knowledge

1. Conformity is a change in a person's opinions or behaviour as a result of real or imagined _pressure_ from a person or group of people.

2. Asch found that conforming to group values reaches a maximum with only ___3___ people.

3. Even if minority influence fails to produce conformity it may still encourage people to _think_ more deeply about the issues in question.

4. Normative conformity can be explained through _punishment_ (the need not to appear naïve or foolish) and reward (acceptance or love).

5. Milgram found that 65% of participants were prepared to give the 'learner' what they thought to be a _450_ volt electric shock.

6. The prison study by Zimbardo was due to last for two weeks but was stopped after ___6___ days because of the effect it was having on participants.

7. When participants are reminded of their responsibility of their own actions then rates of obedience _fall_.

Answers

1 pressure 2 three 3 think 4 punishment 5 450 6 six 7 drop

✓ *If you got them all right, skip to page 42*

Conformity and obedience

20 minutes

Improve your knowledge

1. Society does not have a clear standpoint over whether **conformity** is a good or bad thing. A conformist seems somehow inadequate, a personality-less person, but could also be seen as a team player (a good thing). Nonconformists can be seen as both an individual (a good thing) and a deviant (a bad thing). For example, individuality is not a good thing when driving down the wrong side of the road and a rebellious teenager is not an individual but an anti-conformist, not thinking for him or herself but acting contrary to the expectations of others.

2. Sherif and Asch carried out classic experiments, both of which showed high levels of conformity. However, most people reject the notion that they would conform as the participants did here so we must consider what, if any, factors contributed to the high levels of conformity seen here. Larsen (1974) claimed that it was because of the **social climate** in the US in the 1930s, and the ecological validity of the experiment must also be questioned. However, according to Wolosin et al. (1975) we believe we are motivated by a desire to be correct and others motivated by a desire to be liked. We know that others conform but underestimate the extent to which we do.

3. Although rates of conformity are lower to a minority influence Moscovicki (1985) identified three behavioural styles which are more likely to lead to a minority influence:

   • consistent opposition to the majority
   • a flexible argument
   • an argument consistent with current social trend.

   Nemeth (1986) showed that even if a minority influence fails to produce conformity it may produce other important effects by inducing the majority to think more deeply about the issues in question.

4 In these experiments there are no obvious overt rewards for conforming or punishments for deviance so Aronson (1995) concludes that participants must have been motivated by **normative conformity**. The punishment is the need not to appear to be naïve or foolish and the reward is acceptance or love. In other situations we may only be looking to others for cues as a guide to appropriate actions. For Festinger (1954) we rely on others for **social reality**, not for punishment or reward, but to gain valuable information about what is expected of us.

5 According to Aronson (1995) obedience can be considered as a form of compliance, essentially conforming to a real or perceived authority figure. The Milgram (1963) experiment involved a selection of white- and blue-collar male workers who had volunteered to take part in a study on learning and memory for a small payment. They were tricked into thinking they were the 'teacher' and their co-participant (actually an accomplice of the experimenter) was the 'learner'. The idea was to see how high an electric shock they would give to the learner (in reality no shocks were given) when they answered questions wrongly.

6 Another often quoted study is by Zimbardo et al. (1973). Although the study was researching conformity to social roles, it is relevant to the study of obedience in the way that the prisoners conformed to the authority of the guards to such an extent that 'prisoners' had to be released for various stress related reasons and the study stopped early.

7 There have been several suggestions for why Milgram found such high rates of obedience. His own **'agentic' theory** suggests that we are socialised into this state from a very early age where we accept unquestioningly what we are told to do because most requests seem reasonable and appropriate. However Hamilton (1978) reminded participants that they hold responsibility for their own actions and as a result they developed what Milgram calls an **'autonomous' state** and levels of obedience drop.

Now learn how to use your knowledge

Conformity and obedience

Use your knowledge

1 What are the modifications to Asch's experiment?

consider group size, esteem and status

2 What were the results of Milgram's (1963) study?

how many obeyed?

3 What are the implications of Milgram's work?

blind authority in the military

4 How much influence did the methodology used by Milgram have on the results?

what were the modifications to the 1963 study.

5 What is independent behaviour?

our wish to be unique

6 What is meant by the term 'transfer of responsibility'?

we transfer responsibility f... our actions to those with legitimate powe...

Answers on page 71

Aggressive and helping behaviour

10 minutes

Test your knowledge

1 The Social Learning Theory suggests that aggressive behaviour is learnt by _____ of role models.

2 One source of individual differences in aggressive behaviour may be the tendency we have to _____ hostile intent to others.

3 Punishing children for aggressive behaviour may actually increase the incidence of the unwanted behaviour because paradoxically the punishment is interpreted as a _____.

4 Cognitive strategies for reducing aggressive behaviour try to change the way in which people _____ about frustrating situations.

5 Lab studies often show that in the short term watching aggressive TV can increase the incidence of aggressive behaviour, but these studies lack _____ validity.

6 One situational determinant of bystander apathy is that when more people are present we are _____ likely to help.

7 The Empathy-Altruism Theory of Helping Behaviour suggests that situations which increase empathy result in _____ helping behaviour.

Answers

1 imitation 2 attribute 3 reward 4 think 5 ecological 6 less 7 more

If you got them all right, skip to page 46

43

Aggressive and helping behaviour

20 minutes

Improve your knowledge

1 There are **four social-psychological theories of aggression**. The **Psychoanalytic Theory** put forward by Freud in the late 1800s believed that aggression was due to internal aggressive impulses. Dollard et al. (1939) proposed that the major instigator of aggression is situations viewed as frustrating. Bandura in a series of experiments in the 1960s proposed that aggression could be *learnt* from others and Berkowitz and Lepage (1967) modified the **frustration-aggression hypothesis** to include external cues, the most important of which are those linked to aggression, such as guns and weapons. So over time it can be seen that the theories have moved from viewing aggression as something internal to the individual (Freud and Dollard) to something external to the individual (Bandura and Berkowitz).

2 There are also **Personal-Individual Theories of Aggression** which consider personality factors such as 'type A behaviour', the **Excitation Transfer Theory** which suggests aggression can be triggered by residual physiological arousal and how the process of attribution can influence aggression when we perceive the actions of others as hostile. Gender differences in aggression can be accounted for in biological ways through hormones or through the differing socialisation experiences of men and women.

3 The **Social Psychological Theories of Aggression** provide some clues in reducing aggression. If, as the Social Learning Theory suggests, aggression is learnt, then other *behavioural* methods should reduce aggression. These can include the punishment of aggression, rewarding non-aggressive behaviour and the presence of non-aggressive role models. The most effective behavioural techniques are those which avoid the use of punishment, pain and frustration as these may increase aggression.

4 If aggression is the result of frustration, then **cognitive strategies** may help change the likelihood of an aggressive response to a non-aggressive response. This can include the use of **attitude change techniques** in a counselling or therapeutic capacity and the increase of empathy. Although these techniques are highly effective, they are often difficult to implement as even if convinced that aggression in general is undesirable, individuals will still act aggressively when they believe that it is the best course of action.

5 A number of studies have employed **Bandura's paradigm** using a range of situations and participants, and tend to show that after watching violent TV, aggressive behaviour increases. However, these studies lack ecological validity and only show a short-term effect. One solution would seem to be to use field studies carried out in the natural environment, but generalisations are made difficult by a lack of experimental control.

6 Latane and Darley (1970) proposed a **cognitive model of helping behaviour** based on decisions we ask ourselves before deciding whether to help or not which takes account of many situational factors. Whether we attend to an emergency or not depends on whether we are in a rush or not. Generally we will not perceive an ambiguous situation as an emergency for fear of looking foolish, and due to pluralistic ignorance. Whether we take responsibility for helping depends on the number of people present. If we have specialist training then we are more likely to help and, finally, we weigh up the costs of helping.

7 The **empathy-altruism hypothesis** believes that our helping behaviour is motivated by a desire to help the victim, and consequently emergency situations which increase empathy will also increase helping behaviour. The **empathetic-joy hypothesis** believes that helping behaviour is motivated by the joy experienced when someone else's pain has been alleviated, consequently the higher amount of feedback received will increase helping behaviour.

Now learn how to use your knowledge

Aggressive and helping behaviour

30 minutes

Hints

1 Can aggression be learnt?

do we imitate the actions of behavioural models?

2 What is the experimental evidence for catharsis?

does playing aggressive sports reduce our aggression?

3 Does punishment reduce aggressive behaviour?

how might punishment increase undesired behaviour?

4 What are the proposed effects of watching violent TV?

desensitisation, imitation, arousal

5 What does the correlational study reveal about the relationship between watching aggressive TV and subsequent aggressive behaviour?

are correlationa studies conclusive?

6 What is the Sociobiological Theory of Helping Behaviour?

what is the evolutionary advantage to helping only those with similar genetic material to ourselves?

Answers on page 72

Psychopathology

Test your knowledge

10 minutes

1 Unipolar depression is a _____ disorder with affective, _____, _____ and physical symptoms.

2 Anti-depressant drugs increase levels of various _____ in the brain, particularly dopamine and _____.

3 The Cognitive Theory of Depression suggests that it occurs because of _____ thinking.

4 However, it is open to question whether negative thoughts actually precede negative _____.

5 Schizophrenia is a _____ disorder with _____ and _____ symptoms.

6 Twin and family studies suggest that there is a _____ component to schizophrenia.

7 Abnormally high levels of the neurotransmitter _____ are implicated in schizophrenic symptoms.

8 The evidence for a genetic basis means that few psychologists now believe schizophrenia to be wholly caused by _____ and _____ factors.

9 However, it has been found that a relapse is more likely when the schizophrenic's social environment is high in _____ _____.

 If you got them all right, skip to page 51

Psychopathology

Improve your knowledge

20 minutes

1 **Unipolar depression** is a mood disorder affecting about 4% of the population with four major symptom groups:

Major symptoms of unipolar depression

Symptom group	Symptoms
Affective (mood)	Sadness, irritability, apathy.
Cognitive (thinking)	Low self-esteem, guilt, self-dislike, negative and suicidal thoughts, poor memory.
Behavioural	Loss of appetite, decreased activity, suicide attempts.
Physical	Weight loss, disturbed sleep, lack of energy.

DSM 4 (the manual of psychological disorders) distinguishes between **Major Depressive Disorder** (MDD) which features acute, severe episodes of depression interspersed with normal functioning and **Dysthymic Disorder** (DD) which is chronic (i.e. long term) but has less severe symptoms.

2 The **neurological approach to depression** suggests that it is caused by an imbalance in brain chemistry. Tricyclic drugs used to treat depression affect levels of the neurotransmitters noradrenaline, serotonin and dopamine. Newer drugs (SSRIs) increase serotonin levels only. This may indicate that depression is the result of abnormal serotonin and/or dopamine levels.

Against this view it can be pointed out that:

- post-mortem studies of depressives do not indicate abnormal dopamine levels
- low serotonin levels may have some other cause, such as the low level of motor activity in depressives
- there is no convincing evidence that dopamine levels fall in depressed people.

It is open to question whether the neurological changes cause the psychological symptoms of depression or vice versa.

3 Beck's (1991) **Cognitive Theory of Depression** suggests that it is the result of negative thinking. He proposes that negative views of the self, ongoing experience and the future (called the '**cognitive triad**') interact to interfere with normal motivation and cognitive functioning, resulting in depression.

4 There is some evidence to suggest that depressed people do think in this way. Craighead (1977) found that they tend to recall information in negative terms and recall their failures more often than their successes. However, Davidson and Neale (1992) report that negative thinking occurs after depression has set in and not before. This is contrary to Beck's prediction.

5 **Schizophrenia** is a psychotic disorder affecting about 1% of the population with two major symptom groups:

Major symptoms of schizophrenia

Symptom group	Symptoms
Positive symptoms	Delusions, auditory hallucinations, disorganised speech and behaviour, mood disturbances.
Negative symptoms	Apathy, stupor, bizarre postures, excessive motor activity, anhedonia (inability to enjoy things), echolalia (repeating others' speech).

DSM 4 distinguishes between type one (acute with mainly positive symptoms) and type two (chronic with mainly negative symptoms).

6 **Twin and family** studies indicate that schizophrenia has a hereditary component. That is, people who are closely related to schizophrenics are more likely than the general population to develop the disorder themselves. However, schizophrenia is not 100% heritable. It is likely that it results from an interaction between a **genetic predisposition** and an environmental triggering factor. Possible triggering factors include exposure to a virus and/or to certain types of social environment.

7 **Neurological approaches to schizophrenia** implicate imbalances of neurotransmitters, particularly dopamine (the dopamine hypothesis). Drugs which control the symptoms of schizophrenia, e.g. chlorpromazine, tend to reduce dopamine activity in the brain, and drugs which increase dopamine levels, e.g. amphetamine, can lead to schizophrenia-like symptoms. Post-mortem studies have also indicated high levels of dopamine in the cerebro-spinal fluid of schizophrenics and abnormally high concentrations of dopamine receptors in the caudate nucleus.

8 Various theorists have suggested in the past that schizophrenia is caused by abnormal relationships within the family (**social causation theories**). Due to the weight of evidence in favour of a genetic component to the disorder, these theories have fallen in popularity.

9 However, it has been found that schizophrenics whose symptoms have been controlled are more likely to suffer a relapse if their social environment is high in hostility and criticism (called '**expressed emotion**' or EE). Interventions which aim to reduce the level of EE in the recovering schizophrenic's environment have had some success in reducing relapse rates. Although the EE theory does not explain why people become schizophrenic, it goes some way to explaining why some recover more fully than others.

Now learn how to use your knowledge

Psychopathology

Use your knowledge

Hints

1 Describe unipolar depression.

remember the sub-types

2 Discuss the evidence for a biological cause for depression.

reach a judgement about the evidence

3 What is the 'cognitive triad' and how is it implicated in depression?

compare the theory with the symptoms

4 Explain the difference between positive and negative symptoms in schizophrenia.

use table on p. 49

5 Why do psychologists not think schizophrenia is a genetic disorder?

what would happen if it was?

6 Describe the evidence for the dopamine hypothesis.

look at the actions of drugs

7 Why is the EE model considered more acceptable than the social causation theories?

what does each attempt to explain?

Answers on page 73

Therapies

Test your knowledge

10 minutes

1. Psychoanalytic therapies are based on the idea that psychological problems stem from conflict repressed in the _____ part of the mind.

2. One technique the therapist uses to help clients overcome their problems is _____ of defence mechanisms.

3. Behavioural therapists believe that psychological problems can be attributed to faulty _____ experiences.

4. One technique which is used by both flooding and systematic desensitisation is _____ to the phobic object.

5. The humanistic person-centered approach believes that clients will be in a position to help themselves if the three _____ conditions are provided in therapy.

6. One of the few actual techniques used by the person-centered approach is the provision of _____.

7. Drugs used in the treatment of psychological disorders usually have an effect on levels of _____ in the brain.

8. Electro-convulsive therapy is usually only used nowadays as a last resort for patients suffering from suicidal _____.

Answers

1 unconscious 2 interpretation 3 learning 4 exposure 5 core 6 empathy 7 neurotransmitters 8 depression

 If you got them all right, skip to page 55

Therapies

1 The focus of psychoanalytic therapy rests on the idea that the problem presented by the client is a manifestation of an **unconscious conflict** which has existed in the psyche, potentially since childhood. Therapy is based on removing these repressions rather than treating the symptoms themselves and uses a number of techniques to gain access to these repressed conflicts. **Free association** can facilitate the uncovering of unconscious material. Blocks to free association can indicate where conflicts may exist, as may dream analysis.

2 Unconscious material and defence mechanisms require interpretation by the therapist so that the underlying meaning can be revealed by the therapist. **Transference** is where the client transfers emotional reactions from important people in their lives onto the therapist. This helps to lift repressions and confront deep buried emotions. The therapist must be careful not to allow his or her own emotional reactions to affect their relationship with the client.

3 Therapies derived from the **behaviourist principles** all have one thing in common, that they are all based on the theories of **classical conditioning** (behaviour therapy) or **operant conditioning** (behaviour modification). This means that abnormal responses are learnt just like normal responses. Therapy is based on re-learning appropriate responses.

4 Behaviour therapies, such as **systematic desensitisation**, have been shown to be successful in treating phobias, by a graded exposure to the feared object. **Flooding** is also successful but involves no graded exposure. **Aversion therapy** can be used to remove unwanted behaviours by pairing them with an undesirable response. Techniques of **behavioural modification** have been used to shape the behaviour of autistic children to be more socially appropriate, and token-economy systems have been successfully used to try to reverse some of the effects of institutionalisation on hospitalised chronic mental health patients.

5 Carl Rogers developed the most popular form of **humanistic therapy**, referred to as the **person-centered approach**. With this type of therapy it is the client who is considered to be the expert, unlike all other therapies where it is the therapist. Therapists should not attempt directive or manipulative intervention but create the correct conditions that will help the clients to help themselves. These conditions are genuineness, unconditional positive self-regard and empathy.

6 It is this empathic concern which is considered one of the few actual techniques of humanistic therapy. The therapist restates the emotional aspects of what the client says. This gradually removes emotional blockages because the client can examine them without judgement or disapproval.

7 **Drug therapy** rests on the idea that neurotransmitter function may be linked to mental disorders and so drugs are classed according to the effect they have on the disorder. There are different types of anti-depressants but all raise levels of serotonin and some raise levels of noradrenaline as well. Although there are some nasty side effects, these drugs provide effective short-term relief for depression.

8 **Electro-convulsive therapy** has a controversial history. It is still not clear why it works and in the past it was used as a method for controlling 'problem' patients. Although it is effective for serious depression, nowadays it is only used after all other treatments have failed. Surgery has a similar reputation since lobotomies (cutting of the frontal lobe) were used as a treatment for schizophrenia despite any evidence of its therapeutic value, often leaving only a shell of a person with all personality harshly extracted. On the other hand, commissurotomies, where the *corpus callosum* (the neural pathway which connects the left and right brain hemispheres) is severed, may have had life-saving impact with epileptic patients.

✔ *Now learn how to use your knowledge*

Therapies

Use your knowledge

Hints

1 How effective is psychoanalysis?

2 What are the ethical issues involved in behavioural therapy?

3 How is cognitive-behavioural therapy different from behavioural therapy?

4 What is responsible for client improvement in client-centered therapy?

5 What are the rights of the client in therapy?

6 Which neurotransmitter is linked to schizophrenia?

7 Which neurotransmitter is linked to anxiety?

what are the criteria for success?

is the use of punishment and pain correct?

what is the role of cognition in therapy?

what is the role of the three core conditions?

how much control should the therapist have?

the same neurotransmitter is linked to Parkinson's disease

valium has an effect on this neurotransmitter

Answers on page 73

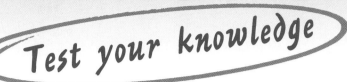

Ethical principles

Test your knowledge

10 minutes

1 The British Psychological Society publishes a _____ of conduct for psychologists to guide research with human participants.

2 Sometimes it is necessary to _____ participants so that they do not know what the aim of the study is.

3 Where there may be some direct consequences for the lives of individuals following a study, research is referred to as _____ sensitive.

4 Some critics have suggested that research into IQ has been used to justify _____ educational policies against some groups.

5 Some psychologists have argued that because the human condition is unique it is not possible to _____ findings from animals to humans.

6 Animals are used in research because it is possible to carry out procedures which would be considered _____ if carried out on humans.

7 One moral argument against animal research is that to inflict _____ is wrong.

8 One way of resolving the debate is to consider the relative costs and _____ of such research.

Answers

1 code 2 deceive 3 socially 4 discriminatory 5 extrapolate 6 unethical 7 pain 8 benefits

 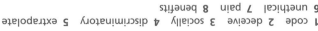

If you got them all right, skip to page 59

Ethical principles

Improve your knowledge

20 minutes

1 The British Psychological Society (1993) published a set of guidelines designed to protect the rights of participants. There are **ten** main points to be considered. Participants must be fully debriefed, should not be deceived, and informed consent should be obtained. Researchers must tell the participants that they have the right to withdraw at any point from the research. The identity of participants and information provided by them must remain fully confidential. Participants should be protected from mental and physical harm. In observational research, where consent has not been obtained, the research should not invade the privacy of participants. The researcher has an obligation to advise participants of any mental or physical problems which become apparent during research, or refer them to a specialist. Finally, all researchers have a responsibility to monitor both themselves and colleagues so that ethical standards can be maintained.

2 There are many examples of research which do not adhere to these principles. Researchers studying helping behaviour often claim that deception of participants is necessary since knowledge of the aims of such research would invalidate the results. This can possibly be justified in that research generally does not cause psychological distress. Where research causes psychological distress or does not gain informed consent the case is harder to justify. Milgram's and Zimbardo's studies have been attacked on these grounds but nevertheless, their methods have been justified by the importance of the results.

3 Nowhere do ethical principles become as closely scrutinised as with **socially sensitive research**. Because of the nature of the research, it may have a direct effect on people's lives, perhaps through social policy, and so it is important that psychologists should be especially cautious when approaching ethical issues.

4 The personal biases of the researcher must be taken into account here so that it is understood that results are not value free. Generally it seems that socially sensitive research is that which may influence public policy such as the gay gene issue and the study for a genetic basis to IQ. Howitt (1991) suggests that psychologists must become more aware of their wider responsibilities.

5 Psychological research with animals rests on the idea that humans and animals are made out of the same 'stuff' and that it is possible to understand the complex 'stuff' of humans by understanding the simpler 'stuff' of animals. Not all psychologists agree with this view however, believing that because the human condition is unique, extrapolating results from animals to humans is not possible.

6 Another argument for the use of animals is that it is possible to carry out procedures with animals which would be considered unethical with humans. Often this involves harming the animal in some way, perhaps permanently through surgery or deprivation.

7 Essentially whether this is a good or bad thing to do is a moral question but an attempt to add some scientific value to the debate has been through judging the extent to which animals can feel pain. The paradox is that the practical argument stresses that we are close enough to animals to extrapolate results to humans but the moral argument stresses that we are not close enough to animals to warrant the same research on humans.

8 One way of resolving the debate is through weighing up the **costs and benefits** of animal research. Bateson (1986) proposed a model, taking into account:

- the quality of research
- the certainty of benefit
- the degree of animal suffering.

So accordingly, if results are of definite benefit to humans then it may be justifiable to cause animal suffering.

Now learn how to use your knowledge

Ethical principles

Use your knowledge

1 Why are Zimbardo's and Milgram's experiments considered to be unethical?

2 What factors could be considered in defence of Milgram and Zimbardo?

3 What type of research could be considered as socially sensitive?

4 Which of the ethical guidelines become especially important when dealing with socially sensitive research?

5 What examples are there of animals used in psychological research?

6 Are there any measures taken to protect animals in psychological research?

Hints

do they break the ethical guidelines of the 1990s?

benefits vs. costs

how might the results of research be used?

which guidelines protect the participant the most?

try perception and biopsychology for good examples

are there guidelines for use of animals?

Answers on page 74

Statistics and research methods

10 minutes

Test your knowledge

1 An experiment involves the manipulation of an _____ variable to see how it affects a _____ variable.

2 An experiment requires two _____ which correspond to changes in the independent variable.

3 During the experiment, all possible _____ variables must be held constant in case they affect the dependent variable.

4 In a _____ study, variables are assessed to see if they co-vary, i.e. if they change in proportion to one another.

5 In an observational study, behaviour is not _____ by the researcher.

6 Before carrying out an observational study, the researcher should produce a behaviour coding scheme to increase the _____ of their observations.

7 Inferential statistics allow researchers to see if relationships between variables are _____.

8 If a set of results is significant, it is unlikely to have been caused by _____.

9 If the researcher accepts that a set of results was significant but they were actually caused by chance, a _____ _____ _____ has occurred.

10 If the wrong statistical test is used to analyse the results, the conclusions reached are likely to be _____.

Answers

1 independent, dependent 2 conditions 3 confounding
4 correlation 5 manipulated 6 reliability 7 significant
8 chance 9 type one error 10 invalid

 If you got them all right, skip to page 65

60

Statistics and research methods

20 minutes

Improve your knowledge

1 In an experiment, the researcher manipulates an **independent variable** (IV) to see how it affects a **dependent variable** (DV). If changes in the dependent variable correspond to changes in the independent variable, it is likely that the two variables are causally linked. That is, changes in the IV are causing changes in the DV.

2 Manipulations of the IV correspond to the two (or more) conditions in the experiment. For example, in an experiment to test the effect of hunger (IV) on perception of pictures of food (DV), in one condition the participants might have eaten recently, whereas in the other condition they might have been deprived of food for a number of hours. A number of different experimental designs can be used to obtain the two conditions.

See the table on the following page.

Experimental designs

Experimental design	Explanation	Advantage	Disadvantage
Independent measures	Different participants used for each condition.	Participants only do the experimental task once, so no practice effects.	Individual differences between the participants (participant variables) can affect results.
Repeated measures	Same participants used for both conditions.	Effect of participants' variables reduced or eliminated.	Repeatedly doing the experimental task can result in improvements due to practice effects.
Matched participants	Different groups of participants, but matched to be as similar as possible (same age, sex etc.).	Participant variables reduced with no risk of practice effects.	Difficult and time consuming to arrrange.

3 **Confounding variables** are variables other than the IV which might cause changes in the DV. They should be held constant (controlled) so that their effect is the same in both conditions.

4 A **correlation study** can tell us if two variables are linked and, if so, how strongly. We can assess correlations using a scattergraph.

Correlation scattergraphs

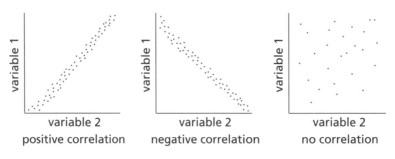

variable 1 / variable 2 — positive correlation   variable 1 / variable 2 — negative correlation   variable 1 / variable 2 — no correlation

We can also use **statistical tests**. These tell us the **correlation coefficient** between the two variables. If the coefficient is close in value to one then the relationship is strong. If it is near zero then there is little or no relationship. If the coefficient is a positive number then as one variable increases, so does the other. If it is negative then as one variable increases, the other decreases.

5 In an **observational study**, the researcher observes behaviour but does not attempt to manipulate it. Observation can be carried out in the lab or the natural environment. In the lab, more control and more detailed observations can be obtained. In the natural environment, behaviour is less likely to be distorted by the artificial surroundings of the lab.

6 A coding scheme for behaviour should be constructed before observations are made. This allows the researcher to decide beforehand how each instance of observed behaviour is to be classified. In an observational study of aggression a coding scheme might be:

Punching	Slapping	Kicking	Verbal abuse

Using a coding scheme increases the reliability of the study: it is more likely that a reliable study can be repeated and the same results obtained.

7 **Inferential statistics** allow researchers to judge whether a set of results was caused by change. If this is unlikely, they are said to be significant.

8 If a set of results is significant it is unlikely to have been caused by **chance**. Inferential statistics allow us to calculate the likelihood of chance results. The less likely it is that results were caused by chance, the more likely it becomes that results were caused by the effect being investigated. Significance is reported as a probability (p) value. A probability value of 0.05 ($p<0.05$) means there is a one in twenty probability that the results arose through chance.

9 Even if statistics show that a set of results is significant, there is still the possibility that they arose by chance. This is because the p-value only tells us how *unlikely* a chance result is, it doesn't tell us that results were definitely caused by the IV. This can lead to errors.

Say the result was caused by the IV when it was caused by chance.	Type one error.
Say the result was caused by chance when it was caused by the IV.	Type two error.

10 The **correct statistical test** should always be used to analyse results or the conclusions reached will be invalid. The type of test used depends on:

- what sort of relationship is being looked for
- what type of data have been obtained
- what sort of experimental design was used.

Type of relationship	Type of data	Type of design	Test to use
Association (to assess whether two variables are linked).	Nominal data (assigning observations to categories).	Independent measures.	Chi-square.
		Repeated measures.	Binomial sign test.
Difference (to assess whether two sets of data are significantly different).	Ordinal (data which can be arranged in rank order).	Independent measures.	Mann-Whitney U test.
		Repeated measures.	Wilcoxon signed ranks test.
Correlation.	Ordinal.		Spearman's Rank-Order correlation.
	Interval (data measured using a scale of measurement e.g. centimetres).		Pearson's product-moment correlation.

Now learn how to use your knowledge

Statistics and research methods

30 minutes

Use your knowledge

Hints

1 A researcher wished to find out how motivation affected concentration. She offered two groups of participants either £1 or £10 to complete a task requiring sustained attention. Participants' scores were recorded.

(a) What experimental design was used?
(b) Why was this a good choice of design?
(c) What were the IV and DV in this experiment?

how many groups?

what might have happened with an alternative design?

2 The researcher analysed her results using a Mann-Whitney U test and found that participants offered £10 scored significantly better than those offered £1 (p<0.01).

(a) Why was a Mann-Whitney U test used?
(b) How likely is it that her results were caused by chance?

there are three reasons

look at the p-value

3 Explain why she is unlikely to have made a type one error.

there is a relationship between significance and type one error

4 The researcher then decided to assess the extent of the relationship between financial incentive and performance on the task. She offered participants between £1 and £10 to complete the task and compared their performance with the amount of money offered to them.

Explain which statistical test should be used to analyse the results.

what sort of relationship is being sought?

5 What ethical difficulties might arise from studies like the two described above?

refer to the section on ethics

✓ Answers on page 75

Answers to Use your knowledge tests

Learning

1. A previously neutral stimulus is paired with a stimulus which already produces a conditioned or reflexive response. After repeated pairings, the neutral stimulus becomes a conditioned stimulus and will produce a response without being paired with the UCS.

2. Pain (UCS) $\rightarrow$ anxiety (UCR)
   Dog (CS) + pain (UCS) $\rightarrow$ anxiety (UCR)
   Dog (CS) $\rightarrow$ anxiety (CR)

3. The variety of human behaviour is too great to be based on a small number of reflexes. Humans actively engage with their environment and do not just respond passively to stimuli.

4. Classical conditioning occurs when two stimuli are presented simultaneously. Operant conditioning occurs due to the consequences a particular behaviour has for the organism which produces it.

5. Behaviours which are followed by a punishment are weakened whereas behaviours which allow an organism to avoid a negative reinforcer are strengthened.

6. Shaping is the selective reinforcement of successively closer approximations of a desired behaviour.

7. Phobics experience anxiety in proximity to their phobic object. If they avoid the phobic object they avoid anxiety, which begins to act as a negative reinforcer. The avoidance behaviour is thus strengthened and the phobia is maintained.

8. SLT relies on observational learning from models. The most effective models to use would be those who are viewed by the largest number of people. Therefore, television programmes could be modified to show more non-aggressive models and more severe consequences for aggressive behaviour.

Perception

1. Another approach is to study children as they grow up and identify which perceptual abilities they learn. Some advances have been made into how children learn to read by using this approach. The alternative approach is to use animals, the rationale being that it is possible to carry out procedures which, whilst ethically questionable in animals, are ethically unacceptable in humans. All of these approaches tend to point to the same conclusion that basic perceptual processes (perception of movement, certain aspects of depth perception) seem to be innate, but fine perceptual discriminations require learning.

2. There are classic studies with human infants by Gibson and Walk (1960) and Bower (1964) and also some animal studies and studies using children aged five to ten years. Critical thinking can include: at what point can it be said that enough experience has taken place so that results cannot indicate depth perception is innate and there are methodological flaws with animal experiments.

3. Eysenck (1993) lists some criticisms. He explains that perception of 3D may involve more factors (we may only perceive a chameleon when it moves) and the laws may not apply to all visual objects especially where similar elements are far apart and dissimilar elements are close together.

4   The left-hand figure of the Müller-Lyer illusion resembles the inside corner of a room and the right-hand figure the outside corner of a box. In these real (3D) circumstances the fins on the right-hand figure are actually further away from the vertical line and on the left-hand figure nearer. However, the rules of size constancy are misapplied to the 2D drawing of the illusion so it follows that if the two vertical lines of the illusion are the same length then the one that is presumed to be further away must be longer in order to throw the same sized retinal image and vice versa.

5   Marr (1982) produced a computational model where he argued that it is more important to address the functions of perception before addressing the mechanisms behind this process. He saw the function of human visual perception as producing information about objects in our environment and produced a three stage model to account for how we build up a picture of our world: a primal sketch, a 2.5D sketch and a 3D sketch.

6   The problem with research into cross-cultural studies is that differences in the way we see illusions may not be due to ecology at all but methodological flaws. It was presumed that all cultures would be able to infer 3D from 2D drawings as we do in the West but in fact not all cultures do this. For some tribespeople the paper the tasks were printed on was more interesting than the task itself and even the tendency to see printed objects as depicting the real world may be a Western phenomenon. So rather than results indicating that different cultures may perceive the world in different ways, results were due to different cultures understanding the tasks in different ways. This shows a Eurocentric approach to psychology, the researchers assuming without question that all cultures would see the task in the same way as Westerners.

Memory

1   There are several research studies which can be seen as evidence for the model:
   * the serial-position effect
   * it appears as if different types of information are used for STM and LTM (coding)
   * brain-damaged patients (the cases of H. M. and C. W.) with anterograde amnesia.

It must be remembered that there are alternative interpretations for this research and it does not necessarily follow that these studies definitely support the multi-store model.

2   The STM as described in the multi-store model cannot do much more than passive processing, such as remembering phone numbers. The working model provides a much more thorough account of the types of active processing we are capable of by linking its function to attention and including other functions such as the visuo-spatial sketch pad.

3   There are a large number of studies which are testament to the effectiveness of organisation at either the encoding or retrieval stage from many different areas of memory study. Studies on categorical clustering give evidence for encoding stage and cue-dependent forgetting for retrieval stage. The experimental work of Collins and Quillan is also relevant here.

4   Bartlett (1932) identified larger units of information called schemata. For example, we all have a restaurant schema in which we store information about the menu, decor, service, etc. (Bower et al., 1979). Bartlett actually showed that our memories do not record information passively like a video tape, but our schemata actually actively reconstruct our memories. Collins and Quillan (1972) developed a model to try to account for how all of these chunks of items are arranged in our LTM. After a series of experiments they suggested that it was organised hierarchically in order to save processing time. The problem with the model was how to account for where the hierarchical part came from and so it was replaced in 1975 with the spreading activation theory by Collins and Loftus who proposed that organisation occurs on the basis of semantic relations (information which is related) but is not hierarchical.

5 Trace decay is when physical memory traces in the brain decay with time. However, it has been shown that the crucial factor is not how much time has passed since learning but what is going on in this period. Certainly it is difficult to explain 'flashbulb memory'. The explanation favoured by most contemporary memory theorists is the context or cue-dependent theory which suggests that in addition to specific information we also tend to store lots of additional information such as our mood state and surroundings at the time of learning. Remembering is a case of getting the cues to trigger off these memories.

6 In order to study practical applications of memory research it might seem obvious to study it in real-life settings but there are problems of experimental control and information about the time and extent of learning. Lab research may be limited because it focuses on retrospective memory whereas everyday memory tends to focus on prospective memory (Wilkins and Baddeley, 1978).

7 A good starting point is the fact that our memory is reconstructive (Bartlett also Carmichael et al., 1932). The lab research by Loftus in the 1970s tends to suggest that since our memories are reconstructive, eye witness testimony is not reliable, whereas the real-life studies suggest that the effects measured by Loftus are not as extreme in real life. The cognitive interview has gone some way to remedying this problem but the Devlin Report recommends that the judge instructs the jury not to convict on a single eyewitness testimony unless supported by substantial corroborative evidence.

Cognitive development

1 The child develops through maturation and experience. Knowledge is organised into schemas through assimilation and accommodation. The child develops in an orderly sequence of stages, with each stage being typified by certain ways of thinking (summarise the table on page 16).

2 Obviously you can't ask the infant if the object continues to exist when it can't be seen. A popular method is to watch the direction of the infant's gaze as it follows an object being moved about. If the object disappears from view on one side of an opaque screen, a child with object permanence will concentrate on the other side, waiting for it to reappear.

3 The main theoretical criticism is that children do not seem to develop in the stop-start fashion predicted by Piaget, but tend to be more steady in their development. The main methodological criticism is that Piaget may have designed tasks that were too hard or lacked 'human sense', leading him to underestimate children's abilities.

4 A stage theory, like Piaget's, but emphasising linguistic and social influences on development. Summarise the stages as in the table on page 17.

5 Piaget tends to view the child as developing in isolation, through its own exploration and discovery of the world. Vygotsky, on the other hand, stresses that cognitive development occurs within a social context and suggests that a child will only fulfil its potential if pushed by a more advanced child or adult.

6 In education, Piaget's ideas led to 'discovery learning' in which a child is supplied with a range of appropriate materials and the time and space to explore them in the expectation that it will develop its cognitive capacities through its own activity. Vygotsky advocates a more structured approach in which the guidance of a more advanced learner is crucial to the fulfilment of the child's cognitive potential.

Moral development

1 Moral development proceeds in stages and each stage consists of a different type of moral reasoning. Describe the stages as in the table on page 20 and stress that moral reasoning is linked to general cognitive development.

2 Piaget's approach stresses the role of internal, maturational factors, i.e. the way the child is capable of more complex thought as it matures, whereas learning theory concentrates on external influences (classical and operant conditioning and observational learning).

3   A number of studies support Piaget's predictions (see, for example, Gross, 1992) but it is important to stress that the vast majority of these were conducted on Western children and hence the results cannot be generalised to children from other cultures.

4   Punishment results in a classically conditioned anxiety response when bad behaviour is contemplated. Parents punish immoral behaviour (and this acts as a negative reinforcer in future) but they also reinforce moral behaviour, for example, with praise.

5   Social Learning Theory, with its focus on the role of observational learning, accounts for the way children may behave morally in novel situations. Traditional Learning Theory requires a person to learn from their own experience, while SLT suggests they can also learn through observing the experiences of others.

6   It could be suggested that the cognitive and learning approaches are not opposed to each other, since they focus on different aspects of morality, moral thinking and moral action respectively. Thus they could be considered complementary to each other.

Evolutionary principles and behaviour

1   Consider what Seligman means by 'biological preparedness'. Animal trainers have found that it is very difficult to teach an animal a behaviour which is not a modification of an existing behaviour. Also consider Koestler's (1970) explanation of insight learning.

2   Many animal behaviours have been explained through fixed action patterns and the related ethological explanation of motivation for these innate behaviours, but these are not without problems. There is an over-reliance on instinctual explanations for behaviour and not all behaviour is easily described by innate releasing mechanisms.

3   A rabbit will thump its hind legs on the ground to warn other rabbits of the presence of a predator whilst at the same time drawing attention to itself. The behaviour appears altruistic but Dawkins (1976) takes a different perspective. At a genetic level the rabbit is increasing the chances of genetic material similar to its own surviving and so is acting in its own self-interest.

4   Evolutionary principles have been applied to many different aspects of animal behaviour. What they all have in common is that they are seeking explanations of animal behaviour based on the idea of adaptiveness to the environment and survival of the fittest. Fighting between many animals of the same species over territory or a mate has become ritualised, whereby disputes are settled with threat and appeasement, dominance and submission. These strategies represent an evolutionary advantage since there is no loss of life.

5   Generally, running speed is a successful characteristic for a predator, but selective pressure may not only favour prey who can run fast, but also other strategies such as living in a large group or camouflage. See Endler's (1991) five stages.

6   Obviously there is only a limited amount of resources available to service a certain number of animals. If resources become limited then some species will stop reproducing. Different species use different strategies which can be dependent on the food type, territoriality and availability.

7   The evolutionary explanation for human mate selection (Kendrick and Keefe, 1992) proposes that there is an evolutionary advantage for males who can pass their genetic material to as many females as possible and an evolutionary advantage for females to choose a male who can provide the best resources for raising offspring. Hence females tend to look for older men with more resources and males look for younger women who are more likely to bear children successfully. Although there is a certain amount of support for this finding (Dunbar, 1995), it does not necessarily follow that the evolutionary explanation is the correct one. The social exchange theory can also equally account

for the findings in terms of social inequalities without making reference to evolutionary principles, but it is near impossible to test. There is a bargaining of the younger woman's youth for the older man's resource. The evolutionary theory also has difficulty in explaining attraction between partners in childless couples and attraction between homosexual partners.

Basic biological processes

1. The nervous system can be divided into CNS, ANS and PNS. The CNS consists of the brain and spinal cord and deals with the processing of information. The brain can be further divided into hind-, mid- and forebrain, all of which contain structures with specialised functions. The ANS is connected to the CNS (via the hypothalamus) and to the internal organs. It is responsible for monitoring and controlling the internal environment, e.g. in homeostasis. It has two branches, the sympathetic and parasympathetic, which become dominant during energy expenditure and conservation respectively. PNS is concerned with the external environment and consists of sensory and motor neurones, which allow sensation and movement.

2. The ANS connects the hypothalamus and the internal organs. It has two branches, the sympathetic and parasympathetic, which work in opposition to each other. The sympathetic branch becomes dominant during energy expenditure and causes heart rate and respiration to increase, stimulates the adrenal medulla to secrete adrenaline and noradrenaline and slows down digestive activity. The parasympathetic branch has the opposite effect. The ANS is involved in a number of functions. In thermo-regulation it has the effect of inducing shivering and the erection of body hairs when the body is too cold, and sweating when it is too hot. The sympathetic branch is responsible for the fight or flight response which, by increasing oxygen intake and glucose release whilst diverting blood to the skeletal muscles, prepares the body for sustained physical activity when faced with a threatening stimulus.

3. Endocrine messages take the form of hormones which are secreted into the bloodstream by the glands of the endocrine system. In contrast to the neural messages sent by the nervous system, this means that they are slower to take effect and affect a wider area than neural messages, with a more sustained action. This can be demonstrated by considering the fight or flight response which has an immediate effect (due to the speed of the sympathetic ANS) but takes a while to die away (because the response is sustained by the hormones adrenaline and noradrenaline).

4. Homeostasis is the mechanism by which the body maintains a stable internal environment. It works by detecting changes and taking appropriate action (feedback). For example, if body temperature rises too far, homeostatic mechanisms produce changes to cause it to fall.

5. The CNS detects changes in body temperature via neurones in the pre-optic hypothalamus. The ANS causes heat to be lost either faster (through sweating) or slower (by erecting body hair) and can cause shivering to increase heat production in the muscles. The endocrine system produces more or less thyroxin to raise (more heat) or lower (less heat) the rate of metabolism.

Sleep and dreaming

1. In birds and reptiles, the light-sensitive pineal gland regulates sleep through the production of melatonin. The pineal gland is also central to the mammalian sleep system but is regulated by the SCN.

2. If we put a human into an environment where there is no day-night cycle, e.g. underground, we would expect them to adjust to a day length of longer than 24 hours, since daylight would no longer be available to reset the SCN.

3. If we connect a person to an EEG and wake them during REM sleep they are more likely to report having dreamed and to provide more detail about the dream's content.

4 Both agree that sleep serves a useful biological function but their emphasis is different. The Restoration theory concentrates on repair and replenishment of the body's tissues whereas the Evolutionary theory emphasises energy conservation.

5 The theories are not mutually exclusive. An Evolutionary theorist would admit that, if an animal is immobilised, this is a good time to undertake repair work; conversely, a Restoration theorist would agree that an animal's evolutionary niche has a major influence on its sleep patterns.

6 Scientists require evidence which can be directly observed. Dreams are subjective insofar as they are available only to the person that has them. The Psychodynamic Theory also relies heavily on the idea of the unconscious, the existence of which cannot be proven either way.

7 Some of the same problems apply to the Activation-Synthesis Theory, particularly those centred around the private nature of dreams. However, the theory does not rely on the existence of the unconscious and fits in with the evidence we have regarding brain activity during REM sleep.

Conformity and obedience

1 If the participants are joined by one ally giving the same answer, conformity drops. If the participant is joined by a non-ally giving a different answer to both the participants and the group, conformity drops. Conformity reaches a maximum in a group of three. Any more than three in a group will not significantly affect conformity. If the participants gave a decision before the group, only 5.7% conformed on hearing the group decision. Those with high self-esteem have a lower conformity rate than those with low self-esteem. This is mediated by task-specific esteem. We will conform less when it is a task at which we feel confident. Increased status of group members will also increase conformity.

2 Psychiatrists predicted that most participants would stop at 150 volts and only 1% would give a 450 volt shock. However, an astonishing 100% of participants gave a 300 volt shock and 65% gave a 450 volt shock which would have been enough to kill. The procedure has been repeated in Australia, Jordan, Spain and West Germany with the same results and there are no gender differences. The experiment has been criticised on ethical grounds (see section on ethics) and because of the methodology which was designed to maximise obedience which would not have occurred in a real-life situation. However, a study by Hofling (1966) showed that this was not the case.

3 According to Aronson (1995) '*An astonishingly large proportion of people will cause pain to other people in obedience to authority. The research may have important counterparts in the world outside of the psychology laboratory*'. The obvious comparison is with Hitler ordering the murder of thousands of innocent civilians. Aronson goes on '*As provocative as these comparisons are, we should be cautious lest we overinterpret Milgram's results*'.

4 There were several factors which maximised rates of obedience. Experiments which have modified Milgram's original procedure have served to highlight some of these. Obedience rates dropped when the study was moved from the prestigious Yale University buildings, when a non-authoritative substitute issued the orders, when the orders were issued down the phone, when participants were forced to hold the learner's arm onto the shock plate and when a fellow teacher defied the demands of the experimenter.

5 This refers to the desire we have to be a unique individual, which may conflict with the desire we have to conform to group norms. The result is that we want to be like others generally but not to the extent that we lose our personal identity. One mediating factor identified by Miller (1992) is our desire for control over our lives – the higher our need, the less we conform. Adorno (1950) suggested that some personality types are prone to authoritarian submission – a tendency to adopt a submissive and uncritical attitude towards authoritarian figures.

6 A similar idea is the transfer of responsibility whereby persons in authority relieve those who obey of the responsibility for their actions. In life situations this may be not be explicit, but in Milgram's experiment it was. Participants were told that the experimenter, not they, would be responsible for the learner's well-being. Legitimate social power is held by authority figures whose role is defined by society, which usually gives them the right to exert control over the behaviour of others. Most people are passive and tend to avoid confrontation, but when exposed to a role model who disobeys the authority of the experimenter, obedience drops (Powers and Geen, 1972). The gradual pressure built up on participants by first giving small and harmless shocks can be avoided by questioning the expertise and motives of the authority figure.

Aggressive and helping behaviour

1 According to behaviourist principles of learning, aggressive responses to frustrating circumstances can be reinforced just like any other behaviour. Bandura proposed that it can also be learnt through imitation. The media demonstrates to children what is expected of them by society. With the widespread TV coverage of events expressing violent solutions to problems, Aronson (1995) believes it is no surprise that children learn that adults often solve their conflicts by resorting to violence.

2 There is a widespread belief that expending aggressive impulses in a socially acceptable form such as exercise will reduce levels of aggression. Patterson (1974) however, showed a significant increase in hostility over the course of a season with US high-school football players. If the catharsis argument was correct then even engaging in actual aggressive behaviour should reduce the need to aggress further, but Geen et al. (1975) showed that the opposite was true. Contrary to the psychoanalytic conception of aggression, increasing aggression does not inhibit the tendency to aggress, it tends to increase it.

3 Punishment can be temporarily effective, but unless used with extreme caution can have the opposite effect in the long term. Parents who use severe punishment with their children may provide a behavioural model for them to imitate. Punishment must avoid frustration to be effective, and on a societal level Eichman (1966) showed that a group of prisoners who had stayed for their full term in jail and 'rehabilitated' were twice as likely to re-offend as another group identical in all respects but released early.

4 The question of whether watching violent TV increases aggression or not has been debated by psychologists since the 1960s, and every few years a high profile case hits the headlines which results in a fresh review of the available literature where a number of studies have contributed suggestions. People's inhibitions to acting aggressively themselves are lowered with repeated exposure to violent TV. According to the excitation-transfer theory the arousal produced by watching violent TV may precipitate aggressive actions by the viewer. Desensitisation to violence occurs when we are repeatedly exposed to violent actions – we stop becoming horrified by it and it becomes part of our everyday norm, thus further violence becomes less objectionable. Bandura proposed that imitation of aggressive role models occurs through the social learning theory. Studies like Gerbner et al. (1980) who showed that children watch five to six violent acts per hour have been cited as cause for alarm but assumes that children are not in a position to discriminate between fiction and real life.

5 Eron and Huesmann (1980) found that those who had watched violent TV at eight years old were still more aggressive at the age of 19 even if they had stopped watching violent TV since that time. However, results are inconclusive and conclusions are likely to reflect personal biases and values rather than a scientific consensus. Aronson (1995) comments '*I would not suggest that watching TV violence is the major antecedent of violence, that would be far too facile. There are many other factors that* *influence aggression, hopelessness, grinding poverty, gangs, drugs and availability of guns. It would also be naïve to deny the influence of the media as a contributory factor.'*

6 The Theory suggests that we will only help others who share similar genetic material to try to protect our own genetic information. This may explain why we help family, but not friends or strangers. The suggestion that we help friends who are genetically similar and can assess a stranger's genetic similarity on the basis of appearance has no supporting evidence.

Psychopathology

1 A mood disorder affecting 4% of the general population. Affective, cognitive, behavioural and physical symptoms. Two subtypes (MDD and DD) with different patterns of severity and duration.

2 The chief evidence for this view is the way anti-depressant drugs can alleviate the symptoms of depression by affecting levels of neurotransmitters. However:
   - drugs are not effective for all people
   - symptoms return if drugs are discontinued
   - abnormalities in brain chemistry may be the result, not the cause of depression.

3 Negative feelings about the self ('I am worthless'), the present ('things are hopeless') and the future ('things will not improve'). Beck suggests that negative cognitions like these affect motivation, hence interfering with cognitive functioning (memory, attention) and emotional experience. This then results in the physical and behavioural symptoms.

4 Positive symptoms, e.g. hallucinations and delusions, are cognitions and behaviours found in schizophrenics which are not usually found in clinically normal people. Negative symptoms, e.g. apathy and anhedonia, refer to behavioural deficits, that is, they refer to things found in clinically normal people but not in schizophrenics.

5 Whilst genetic relatives of schizophrenics have a higher risk of developing schizophrenia than the general population, the disorder is not 100% genetic in origin. Twin studies show that if one monozygotic twin develops schizophrenia, the other does so in about 48% of cases. Since MZ twins have identical genetic material, a wholly genetic disorder would result in both twins inevitably developing schizophrenia. Since this is not the case, there must be at least one other factor at work in the origin of schizophrenia.

6 Neuroleptic drugs, which can control the symptoms of schizophrenia, tend to do so by blocking dopamine neurotransmission in the brain. High levels of dopamine have been found in post-mortem studies of schizophrenics. Drugs which artificially increase dopamine levels, e.g. amphetamines and L-Dopa, can produce a psychotic reaction in clinically normal people similar to schizophrenia. This can be reduced through the use of neuroleptics.

7 The social causation theories of schizophrenia have lost their weight due to the increasing evidence for a genetic basis to schizophrenia. The EE model has become popular because:
   - it provides an indication as to what the triggering factor in schizophrenia may be
   - it is still able to accommodate the genetic evidence
   - it provides a workable therapeutic intervention to prevent relapse.

Therapies

1 The principal problem in evaluating the effectiveness of psychoanalysis is in how success is measured, since it is virtually impossible to test empirically if unconscious conflicts have been removed or not. Consequently, most studies use symptom removal as a measure of success and it is suggested that for neurotic clients psychoanalysis may not be any more effective than the improvement made over the passage of time. Eysenck (1952) reviewed 24 studies and concluded that psychoanalysis is no more effective than no therapy at all. In a 1992 review he reached the same conclusion. This may be due to the criteria used for success, it may not be appropriate to use the same criteria for psychoanalysis as behavioural therapy (symptom removal). Luborsky and Spence (1978) summarise some of the limitations of psychoanalysis.

2 Marks et al. (1970) showed homosexual men pictures of nude males paired with electric shocks and reported that, in some cases, homosexual response decreased. This poses three questions: do psychologists have the right to choose what is right and wrong? Do psychologists have the right to choose how others will behave? And do psychologists have the right to inflict pain on others?

3 Cognitive-behavioural therapy is a distinct form of therapy. Rational-emotive therapy developed by Albert Ellis (1973) places the emphasis of therapy on identifying the irrational thought processes of clients and seeking to replace them with rational ones.

4 Lambert et al. (1986) believe that it is not actually the three core conditions that are responsible for client improvement but they create an atmosphere of trust and safety in which clients are encouraged to explore aspects of themselves and this is what is responsible for client improvement. This type of therapy has become a very popular counselling technique, but rather than proving useful for specific disorders it represents a general approach to building up a trusting relationship with a client which many therapists from different traditions have used.

5 Along with ethical considerations there are several issues which need to be dealt with including:
- confidentiality (should the therapist inform police of illegal activities?)
- informed consent (should the client be informed of potential harm?)
- choice of treatment (should sectioned patients have the right to refuse medication?)
- choice of goals (should the therapist set goals against the wishes of clients?).

6 Phenothiazines are used to treat schizophrenia by reducing the synaptic activity of dopamine. These drugs are not effective for all types of schizophrenia and produce some very serious side effects (similar to Parkinson's disease) for approximately 30% of patients on long-term medication.

7 Benzodiazepines such as Valium are used to treat anxiety disorders by working on specific receptors which in turn reduce serotonin activity. Although they may provide short term relief, continuous use may lead to dependence. Drug therapy is a very popular approach with the medical profession but in the past there has tended to be an over-reliance on this method.

Ethical principles

1 Milgram's experiment involved deceiving participants as to the nature of the study, not informing participants of their right to withdraw from the experiment and causing psychological distress. Baumrind (1964) criticised Milgram, believing that he did not take sufficient measures to protect his participants. Zimbardo faced similar criticisms, from Savin (1973), that participants were deceived, that participants did not give fully informed consent (they did not know the full procedure) and that participants were humiliated and dehumanised.

2 Both Milgram and Zimbardo defended their research by suggesting that these measures were necessary in order for the situations to be considered real and that the means justified the ends, in terms of the benefit gained from such knowledge. Both researchers carried out extensive post-experimental debriefing and follow-up research and Milgram also claimed that in advance he could have not predicted how far participants would have obeyed. In a pilot study it was estimated that very few participants would continue beyond half-way.

3 Any research which may have a direct effect on people's lives, especially where it is used for discriminatory purposes. There are substantial implications on people's lives of research considering the genetical bases of homosexuality, intelligence, addictive personality, etc. There is a fear that this research could be used to justify discrimination against these groups. Other types of research may be used to influence public policy and even law.

4 Sieber and Stanley (1988) highlight several ethical principles which are particularly important in socially sensitive research.

   (a) Special attention should be paid to privacy and confidentiality since data may be used for reasons other than that for which it was originally intended. This raises the issue of who 'owns' the data; the public, the psychologist or the participant?

   (b) Research must have a sound and valid methodology so that results are not easily misunderstood or manipulated by the public and media.

   (c) Considering the nature of this type of research it is important that researchers obtain the informed consent of participants and avoid deception.

   (d) All procedures should involve justice and equitable treatment and the interests of society must be carefully balanced against the advance of science.

5 Hubel and Wiesel (1962) implanted electrodes in the brains of cats to identify areas of cortical functioning responsible for perception. Although this involved destruction of brain tissue, the fact that they received a Nobel Prize in 1981 implies that their use of animals was justified. Jouvet (1967) used the 'flowerpot' technique to study the effects of REM. Cats were subjected to suffering and they all died after approximately 21 days. The flowerpot technique is unreliable and did not add crucially to the development of sleep research and so in retrospect is difficult to justify. Other studies to consider are Harlow (1959) and Seligman (1975).

6 The British Psychological Society and the Experimental Psychology Society jointly issued some guidelines in 1993 in which researchers must not use excessively painful procedures.

Statistics and research methods

1 (a) Independent measures.
   (b) Repeated measures might have resulted in practice or order effects.
   (c) IV was the amount of money offered, DV was the participant's score on the task.

2 (a) Mann-Whitney is appropriate when a difference is sought, data are at least ordinal level and an unrelated design, i.e. independent measures, is used.
   (b) The likelihood of these results occurring by chance is 1 in 100.

3 The smaller the p-value, the less likely it is that the results occurred by chance. Therefore at smaller p-values there is less chance of the researcher accepting a set of chance results as significant.

4 She is looking to see whether a rise in one variable is accompanied by a rise in another (a correlation). Both variables are measured on a scale with equal units (interval level data) therefore Pearson's Product-Moment is appropriate.

5 Both the studies involve payment to participants which may make them feel obliged to continue with the study even if they don't want to.

Select bibliography

Learning
Bandura, A. (1973). Aggression: a social learning analysis. London: Prentice Hall.
Pavlov, I. P. (1927). Conditioned Reflexes. London: Oxford University Press.
Skinner, B. F. (1938). The Behavior of Organisms. New York: Appleton-Century-Crofts
Watson, J. B. (1919). Psychology from the standpoint of a behaviorist. Philadelphia: J. B. Lippincourt
Watson, J. B. and Rayner, R. (1920). Conditioned emotional reactions. *Journal of Experimental Psychology*, 3, 1–14.

Perception
Bower, T. G. R. (1964). Discrimination of depth in premotor infants. Psychonomic Science, 1368.
Dallenbach, K. M. (1951). A picture puzzle with a new principle of concealment. *American Journal of Psychology*, 64, 431–3.
Eysenck, M. W. (1993). Principles of cognitive psychology. Hove: Lawrence Erlbaum Associates.
Gibson, E. J. and Walk, R. D. (1960). The visual cliff. *Scientific American*, 202, 64–71.
Gibson, J. J. (1979). The ecological approach to visual perception. Boston: Houghton Mifflin.
Gregory, R. L. (1972). Seeing as thinking. *Times Literary Supplement*, 23 June.
Koffka, K. (1935). Principles of gestalt psychology. New York: Harcourt Brace.
Marr, D. (1982). Vision: A computational investigation into the human representation and processing of visual information. San Francisco: Freeman.
Neisser, U. (1976). Cognition and Reality. San Francisco: Freeman.
Segall, M. H., Campbell, D. T. and Herskovits, M. J. (1966). The influence of culture on visual perception. Indianapolis: Bobbs-Merrill.

Memory
Bartlett, F. C. (1932). Remembering: A study in experimental and social psychology. Cambridge: Cambridge University Press.
Bower, G. H., Black, J. B. and Turner, T. J. (1979). Scripts in memory for text. *Cognitive Psychology* 11, 177–220.
Carmichael, L. M., Hogan, H. P. and Walter A. A. (1932). An experimental study of the effect of language on the reproduction of visually perceived forms. *Journal of Experimental Psychology*, 15, 137–160.
Collins, A. M. and Quillan, M. R. (1969). Retrieval time from semantic memory. *Journal of Verbal Learning and Verbal Behaviour*, 9, 432–438.
Eysenck, M. W. (1977). Human Memory: Theory research and individual differences. Oxford: Pergammon.
Miller, G. A. (1965). The magic number seven, plus or minus two: Some limits on our capacity for processing information. *Psychology Review*, 63, 81–93.

Cognitive development
Piaget, J. (1954). The Construction of Reality in the Child. New York: Basic Books.
Vygotsky L. S. (1934). Thought and Language. Translated by E. Hanfman and G. Vakar (1962). Cambridge, Massachusetts: MIT Press.

Moral development

Chandler, M. J., Greenspan, S. and Barenboim, C. (1973). Judgements of intentionality in response to videotaped and verbally presented moral dilemmas: the medium is the message. *Child Development*, 44, 315–320.

Piaget, J. (1932). The Moral Judgement of the Child. Harmondsworth: Penguin.

Evolutionary principles

Dawkins, R. (1976). The Selfish Gene. Oxford, Oxford University Press.

Dunbar, R. I. M. (1989). Genetic similarity theory needs more development. *Behavioural and Brain Sciences*, 12, 520–1.

Endler, J. A. (1991) Interactions Between Predators and Prey in J. R. Krebs and N. B. Davies (Eds) Behavioural ecology: An evolutionary approach. 3rd ed. Oxford: Blackwell.

Kendrick, D. T. and Keefe, R. C. (1992). Age preferences in mates reflect sex differences in human reproductive strategies. *Behavioural and Brain Sciences*, 15, 75–133.

Koestler, A. (1970). The Act Of Creation. London: Pan Books.

Rushton, J. P. (1989). Genetic similarity, mate choice and fecundity in humans. *Ethology and Sociobiology*, 9, 329–33.

Sherry, D. F. and Galef, B. G. (1984). Cultural transmission without imitation: milk bottle opening by birds. *Animal Behaviour*, 32, 937–8.

Tinbergen, N. and Perdeck, A. C. (1950) On the stimulus situation releasing the beginning behaviour in the newly hatched herring-gull chick. *Behaviour*, 3, 1–39.

Basic biological processes

Kalat, J. W. (1998). Biological Psychology (6th ed.). Pacific Grove, California: Brooks/Cole.

Conformity

Adorno, T. W., Frenkel-Brunswick, E., Levison, D. J. and Sandford, R. H. (1950). The authoritarian personality. New York: Harper and Row.

Aronson, E. (1995). The Social Animal. New York: Freeman.

Festinger, L. (1954). A theory of social comparison processes. *Human Relations* 7, 117–140.

Hamilton, G. V. (1978). Obedience and responsibility: A jury simulation. *Journal of Personality and Social Psychology*, 26, 121–146.

Hofling, C. K., Brotzman, E., Dalrymple, S., Graves, N, and Pierce, C. M. (1966). An experimental study in nurse-physician relationships. *Journal of Nervous and Mental Disorders*, 142, 171–180.

Larsen, K. S. (1974). Conformity in the Asch experiment. *Journal of Social Psychology*, 94, 303–4.

Milgram, S. (1963). Behavioural study of obedience. *Journal of Abnormal and Social Psychology*, 67, 371–8.

Moscovicki, S. (1985). Social influence and conformity. In G. Lindzey and E. Aronson (Eds) Handbook of Social Psychology. 3rd ed. New York: Random House.

Nemeth, C. J. (1986). Differential contributions of majority and minority influence. *Psychological Review*, 93, 23–32.

Wolosin, R., Sherman, S. and Cann, A. (1975). Predictions of own and others' conformity. *Journal of Personality*, 43, 357–8.

Zimbardo, P., Banks, P. G., Hanaey, C. and Jaffe, D. (1973). A Pirandellian prison. *New York Times* magazine 814173.

Aggression

Aronson, E. (1995). The Social Animal. New York: Freeman

Berkowitz, L. and LePage, A. (1967) Weapons as aggression-eliciting stimuli. *Journal of Personality and Social Psychology*, 11, 202–7.

Dollard, J., Doob, L., Miller, N. E., Mowrer, O. H. and Sears, R. (1939). Frustration and aggression. Newhaven: Yale University Press.

Eichmann, C. (1966). The impact of the Gideon decision on crime and sentencing in Florida. Tallahassee, FL: Division of corrections publications.

Eron, L. R. and Huesmann, R. (1980). Adolescent aggression and television. Annals of the New York Academy of Sciences.

Geen, R., Stonner, D. and Shope, G. (1975). The facilitation of aggression by aggression: A study in response inhibition and disinhibition. *Journal of Personality and Social Psychology*.

Gerbner, G., Gross, L., Signorielli, N. and Morgan, M. (1980). Television violence, victimization and power. *American Behavioural Scientist*, 23, 705–16.

Latane, B. and Darley, J. M. (1970). The unresponsive bystander: Why doesn't he help? New York: Appleton Century Crofts.

Psychopathology

Beck A. T. (1991). Cognitive Therapy: a 30-year retrospective. *American Psychologist*, 46 (4), 368–375.

Therapies

Ellis, A. (1973). Humanistic Psychotherapy. New York. McGraw Hill.

Eysenck, H. J. (1952). The effects of psychotherapy: an evaluation. *Journal of Consulting Psychology*, 16, 319–24.

Eysenck, H. J. (1992). The outcome problem in psychotherapy. In W. Dryden and C. Feltham (Eds) Psychotherapy and its discontents. Buckingham: Open University Press.

Lambert, M. J., Shapiro, D. A. and Bergin, A. E. (1986). The effectiveness of psychotherapy. In S. L. Garfield and A. E. Bergin (Eds) Handbook of Psychotherapy and Behaviour Change: An empirical analysis (3rd ed.). New York: Wiley.

Luborsky, I., and Spence, D. P. (1978). Quantitative research on psychoanalytic therapy. In S. L. Garfield and A. E. Bergin (Eds) Handbook of Psychotherapy and Behaviour Change: An empirical analysis (2nd ed.). New York: Wiley.

Marks, I. M., Gelder, M. and Bancroft, J. Sexual deviants two years after electric aversion. *British Journal of Psychiatry*, 117, 173–85. (1970).

Ethics

Bateson,P. (1986). When to experiment on animals. *New Scientist*, 109, 30–2.

Baumrind, D. (1964). Some thoughts on the ethics of research: after reading Milgram's behavioural study of obedience. *American Psychologist*, 19, 421–3.

British Psychological Society (1993). Code of conduct, ethical principles and guidelines. Leicester: BPS.

Harlow, H. F. (1959). Love in infant monkeys. *Scientific American*, 200 (6), 68–74.

Howitt, D. (1991). Concerning psychology, Psychology applied to social issues. Milton Keynes: Open University Press.

Hubel, D. H. and Wiesel, T. N. (1959). Receptive fields of single neurons in the cat's striate cortex. *Journal of Physiology*, 160, 106–54.

Jouvet, M. (1967). Mechanisms of the states of sleep: A neuropharmacological approach. Research publications of the association for the research in neurons and mental diseases, 45, 86–126.

Savin, H. B. (1973). Professors and psychological researchers: Conflicting values in conflicting roles. *Cognition*. 2 (1), 147–9.

Seligman. M. E. P. (1975). Helplessness. On development, depression and death. San Francisco: W. H. Freeman.

Sieber, J. E. and Stanley, B. (1988). Ethical and professional dimensions of socially sensitive research. *American Psychologist*, 43 (1), 149–55.